TAAI

An Inspiring Journey
as Former Lok Sabha Speaker
Padma Bhushan Sumitra Mahajan

AF552789

TAAI

An Inspiring Journey
as Former Lok Sabha Speaker
Padma Bhushan Sumitra Mahajan

Medha Kirit

Translation

Sharmila Bhagwat

PRABHAT
PAPERBACKS

No part of this publication can be reproduced, stored in a retrieval system or transmitted in any form or by any means, electronic, mechanical, photocopying, recording or otherwise, without prior permission of the author. Rights of this book are with the author.

Published by
PRABHAT PAPERBACKS
An imprint of Prabhat Prakashan Pvt. Ltd.
4/19 Asaf Ali Road,
New Delhi-110002 (INDIA)
e-mail: prabhatbooks@gmail.com

ISBN 978-93-5521-082-1
TAAI
by Smt. Medha Kirit

© Reserved

Edition
First, 2022

Price
₹ 300.00 (Rupees Three Hundred only)

Printed at
R-Tech Offset Printers, Delhi

Dedicated to
patriotic youth
committed to
the social cause.

Foreword

Dear Medha Kirit Somaiya has heartily penned down my journey and contributions as the Speaker of Lok Sabha, at times even glorifying me!

However, when I look back, I cannot resist admitting that I was competent enough and even had the vigour to excel in whatever I took up! The problems faced by women was like a festering sore for me and preoccupied my mind. I ponder over it even now.

I had acquired sufficient knowledge about many subjects, but all this would count if given an opportunity. It is said:

'अमन्त्रम् अक्षरं नास्ति नास्ति मूलम् अनौषधम्
अयोग्यः पुरुषो नास्ति योजकः तत्र दुर्लभः !!'

(There is no sound that is not a *mantra*, no plant that is not medicinal. There is no person unworthy, but what is rare is an enabler or a connector!)|

And that is what happened in 2014. Hon'ble Prime Minister Narendra Modiji was an unusual planner who gave me a chance, an opportunity to flourish by providing a platform to showcase my abilities to the world. It was indeed a huge opening!

It is true that the Bharatiya Janata Party (BJP) had remained in the Opposition most of the time, particularly before I became a member of the Lok Sabha. The BJP was in power just for 13 days in 1996 and later for 13 months in

1998, under the leadership of Atal Bihari Vajpayee. But when the BJP government came to power with a thumping victory in 1999, Jayawantiben Mehta and me were given the chance to become Ministers of State. In fact, we were quite senior and experienced at the time as we had worked for the party for many years and had experience as Members of Parliament for four to five terms. Considering our experience, we could have become even Cabinet ministers! Of course, we weren't upset or distressed about it! However, in hindsight I feel that we may have proved better as Cabinet ministers then.

Nonetheless, Hon'ble Murli Manohar Joshi, who was the Union Human Resources Development Minister, gave me the freedom to take many important decisions as a Union Minister of State in the Ministry of Women and Child Development. He always supported and encouraged me. Given a free hand, I decided to double the honorarium of *Anganwadi* workers and instituted state-level and national-level awards for them. I initiated distribution of five national 'Stree Shakti' awards. I also conducted many seminars on women's issues. After a very active period of two-and-a-half years, I was appointed the Minister of State for Communications and finally as the Minister of State for Petroleum.

We, as members of the BJP, had to sit in opposition after the elections of 2004. Later I often heard comments that senior leaders like Hon'ble L.K. Advaniji often praised me saying, "Sumitra is smart. She is senior, experienced and quite studious," and so on. Sometimes I wondered that if he really considered me intelligent, then why was I not included in the National Executive Committee or given the opportunity to speak on an important proposal or state subject in the Lok Sabha? Of course, my name was often mentioned regarding women-related issues, but I could not fathom why I was not made the principal speaker on other important topics. Such thoughts used to trouble my mind very often then. But then,

I was aware of my weakness – not adopting an aggressive attitude. Aggression is perhaps a necessary quality to employ in today's politics but it was not in my nature to forge ahead through force. I never believed in pushing myself ahead of others.

I was seeped in the ethos of the Rashtriya Swayamsevak Sangh and Rashtra Sevika Samiti. The principles of RSS had been nurtured in me since my childhood. To attend a Samiti *shakha* was a diktat in my house. Many cultural events and activities were organised in my home town, Chiplun. Vasant Vyakhyanmala was a significant event to attend and which my father encouraged. Thus, this gave me the golden opportunity to listen to some great orators during my childhood. I participated in many competitions in the school as well. The fresh and open atmosphere encouraged me to display my talents lying hidden so far. In 1959, when I was in Standard XI, my father passed away, leaving us to lead a life of penury. Life became very tough for all my siblings for the next five to six years as it meant having to earn to learn. I started to work at the Accountant General's office.

However, my life underwent a change when I got married and came to Indore. My husband was very supportive and took interest in a variety of activities. Moreover, my in-laws not only loved and cared for me but encouraged me to complete my studies. As if God had showered his blessings on me, their words still ring in my ears: "Do whatever you like." And yes, since then I have never looked back. It's been an upward journey, always!

Initially, I accompanied my mother-in-law to the Mahila Mandal, but subsequently I started attending the RSS *shakha* (daily meeting) of Rashtra Sevika Samiti (the female wing of the RSS) as also literary meets, elocution contests, *Sanskar Vargas*, and gradually the list began to grow longer and longer. I used to attend the *shakha* for adults once a week. That was when my mother-in-law cautioned me, "You can do whatever you want, but always remember to return home before Jayant (my husband) returns from work. I will manage once in a while but this shouldn't happen always!" So I religiously tried to balance home and outside activities.

I was the youngest member in the Samiti and also the most daring as I could ride both a bicycle and a scooter. The inspiring life-stories of Jijabai, Ahilyabai and Rani of Jhansi were narrated to teach how they were embodiments of motherhood, competence-efficiency and leadership in the Samiti. We, the *sevikas*, were encouraged to speak at various events and were duly trained in extempore speaking. Mainatai Gokhale, the head of the Samiti, was the sister of the venerable Lakshmibai Kelkar 'Mavshi' (the founder of the Samiti). She was an accomplished orator and well known for her scholarly pursuits. I learnt from her the art of delivering *pravachanas* (religious discourses) on the *Ramayana*. Vatsalatai Namjoshi also introduced many novel activities. She had a good command over the Hindi language, the nuances of which I picked up from her. Gradually, I started giving discourses in Hindi as well.

Every year, we visited the ruler's palace area on the death anniversary of Ahilyabai to offer her a garland on behalf of the committee, wearing the uniform of the Samiti. We would recite the stotras in Hindi penned by Hon'ble Vatsalatai. There were many other people, but we would return back after reciting stotras and aarti, the tradition continues even today. I do visit the place even now, wearing Samiti uniform.

Thanks to Rashtra Sevika Samiti, I could study the character of Punyashlok Ahilyadevi in great details. Her fair and just rule and her noble work at various places of pilgrimages in the country inspired me a lot. I clearly remember, before delivering my Pravachan I always maintained, "I do not speak in front of you as a scholar but before delivering every lecture,

I read more and more about the queen and I get acquainted with new aspects of her character every time. I get mesmerized by her personality. I get engrossed in the character. It leaves a strong impression on my mind, and that is the purpose of my discourses."

The Noble ruler who had rare social and political acumen Ahilyamata left so deep impression on my mind that I did not even realise when simplicity, honesty, uprightness and dedication became my goals in social as well as political life.

With unwavering faith and conviction, I went on accepting every challenge in life.

The imposition of Emergency jolted me, I was not content being a fence sitter in the face of injustice. I had to fight it... Thus I plunged into politics. But I continued to serve Goddess Ahilyabai Holkar In 1981, I took charge of the Women's Conference as a member of the Ahilya Committee, then became a Women's Representative and from 1984 to 1986 was a Joint Secretary. In 1994, I became the chairman of the Ahilya festival committee. And the responsibility continues till today. We all are striving hard to fulfill our duty. The work has expanded manifold. In 1996, we celebrated the 200th birth anniversary of Mother Ahilyabai in a big way.

The committee constituted Devi Ahilyabai National Award. The first award was presented to social reformer Nanaji Deshmukh by then Prime Minister of the country Atal Bihari Vajpayee and since then many distinguished personalities have been honored by many celebrities. We are fortunate that the good work continues even today.

It was my good fortune to get good mentors in my political journey in the form of Hon'ble Kushabhau Thakre and Rajmataji Vijayaraje. Hon'ble Kushabhau's own life was so ideal and transparent, that no one had to teach us "karmanyevadhikaraste ma faleshu kadachan'! Honorable Kushabhau would never praise openly. It was through somebody that we would know his compliments. There was an incident—The topic of discussion was giving chance to women. A senior party worker said, "Kushabhau, by bringing Sumitrataai we have given 100% opportunity to women. Kushabhau immediately remarked, "Look, it's not because you gave her the chance, but she has achieved the position on her merits. Do not take any unnecessary credit. "I was on cloud nine ever since I came to know about the compliment!"

I always remained closely associated with the Rashtra Sevika Samiti. I continue to get phone calls from hon'ble Pramilatai regularly assuring, "not to worry at all, we all are there with you". She would praise me for the appropriate decision. Otherwise she would ask, 'why did you do this'? Or 'why were you angry so much'?" And after knowing everything would say with a laugh, "ok ok don't worry, I ask all this so that nobody should point a finger at our girl/sevika and say that she erred."

It is really my good fortune that I am blessed with a strong group of dedicated, efficient and honest office associates in Indore as well as Delhi. By experience, they can very well understand my requirements and thoughts in my mind and start working in the direction. Even now they are all ready and prepared to help me. This is indeed the blessing of almighty!

With all the protection around me, why should I worry? The confidence and trust Modiji showed on me by bestowing the responsibility of the Speaker of the Lok Sabha. Now I can very well say that I endured it with self-respect and confidence.

—Sumitra Mahajan

Preface

'Padmabhushan' Sumitratai Mahajan...

Former Speaker of Lok Sabha!

An ordinary girl from Chiplun village in Konkan who entered in politics for social service and remained active in politics from 1984 to 2019!! With her intelligence, perseverance and hard work surpassed all the challenges and became the highest authority of the Lok Sabha.

The book portrays the wonderful journey of Sumitrataai Mahajan as a speaker of Lok Sabha and highlights her selected contributions. An ordinary middle class housewife gets elected to the Lok Sabha eight times in a row from same political party-BJP, from Indore and later is unanimously elected as the Speaker of the Lok Sabha. Taai is indeed an exceptional illustration of an extraordinary talent! I felt it essential to depict the making of the amazing personality and offer a glimpse of her manifold work at the supreme position. My prayers were fruitful and Sumitrataai agreed for the venture. It was decided to concentrate on her inspiring work as the Speaker of the 16th Lok Sabha from 2014-2019. Her cooperation and guidance was invaluable, right from the conception to completion of the book. The book attempts to present certain significant incidents in her career as a Lok Sabha Speaker before the general public, with her consent.

Each chapter of the book contains the relevant quotation of Saint Samarth Ramdas on the concerned subject. Maharashtra is blessed with the great tradition of saints and the contribution of Samarth Ramdas is quite significant in it. Ramdas Swami was a great saint, philosopher, poet and social reformer who perfectly blended the spiritual and practical sides of life and emphasized the importance of one's duty and ingenuity. He was a devotee and a follower of Lord Rama and Lord Hanuman and stressed on the physical strength and exercise of individuals. He built temples of Hanuman and gyms at various places - villages. He was of the opinion that saints must not withdraw from society but instead actively engage towards social and moral transformation.

When society was stressed and frightened Ramdas Swami did the important work of awakening masses, uniting them, created awareness among women and stressed the importance of women's education. Ramdas Swami's distinct work -Dasbodh, guides one to utilise the rare opportunity of the human life to live life meaningfully and pursue the purpose of human life. Taai is the great follower of Samarth Ramdas Swami and his philosophy has a great influence on her life; it somehow reflects in her personality. Even today, if Taai feels disturbed or distressed she turns to Dasbodh for solace and inspiration. That is why the verses are relevant and significant in Taai's journey.

Determination, efficiency and mental strength are Taai's significant characteristics. Taai lost her mother when she was in fourth standard her father died when she was in eleventh standard. She had to stay with her relatives in Mumbai to continue her education. She also secured a job for herself in the office of Accountant General. She came to Indore after marrying Late Advocate Jayant Mahajan. Due to her upbringing and sanskars of Rashtriya Swayamsevak Sangh and Rashtra Sevika Samiti, she became active in social work in Indore. With the support and encouragement from her in-laws and her husband she earned her master's degree and also completed her law. And later rose to the highest position of the speaker of the Indian Parliament, one of the largest democracies in the world.

Taai believed in three innate qualities of women—motherhood, competence, and leadership and clearly asserted that women should not demand, argue or plead for their rights but society should offer them to her with respect. Taai always believed more in action than mere talk and gained a firm foothold in Madhya Pradesh for 40 years, in a patriarchal and dynastic-dominated field of politics.

Taai endured the principles of honesty, sincerity, simplicity and faith in public life. She followed the footsteps of her idol Punyashlok Ahilyabai Holkar. She is well-known for her 'lady next door' image. She lived up to the image. Sober and sedate Taai had to face many ups and downs in the life. All of a sudden she lost her husband, her greatest strength in life. But she maintained her poise in public life. This, however, is not to suggest that she did not have to face political antagonism and competitions. But she treads her own path. With the strong shield of public support, she could face the situation successfully.

I always had a great fascination and respect for Taai. I am fortunate to have a close association with Taai for many years. She had also written introduction to my book in Marathi 'Sakhi Sutra'. As my husband Dr. Kirit Somaiya is the BJP leader, I have interacted with her on many occasions while working for Kamal Sakhi Manch and she was always ready to help. When I voiced the thoughts regarding a book, Taai agreed for the depiction of the journey as a Speaker of the Lok Sabha. Accordingly, the book details her distinct work as the speaker of the Lok Sabha in 16 chapters and tries to seek how it was possible for her and in the process also reveals some strong traits of her character.

It portrays her feelings—varied emotions. The 9th chapter depicts her unwavering faith in Devi Ahilyabai. The book reveals how her sensitive mind captured various cultural traditions while travelling within the country and abroad. It contains her thoughts on international affairs while taking a review of constitutional reforms while demarcating India-Bangladesh border. It also mirrors her sadness and despair at the death of Shri E Ahamed. It details information about Speakers Research Initiative and her thoughts on women over the years.

Many people have contributed to this endeavor. The book also includes views of Taai's colleagues, associates, friends and employees. It reflects their deep affection and respect or Taai who are 'ever ready to do anything for Taai'! This is indeed Taai's treasure that is precious and priceless.

Taai's love and passion for languages is well-known. She has a great penchant for diverse literature, tradition and culture. She is well-versed in English, Hindi, Marathi and Sanskrit. 'Taai' was published in Marathi in April 2022. It was translated in Hindi in May 2022. The need was felt to publish the book in English also. I am grateful that Prabhat Publications agreed to publish the book in English. Senior journalist Sharmila Bhagwat has striven hard to maintain the spirit and style of the original manuscript while translating the book in English. The language is simple, lucid and effective.

'Taai' can inspire not only women but anyone who wants to achieve his goals in life. If they are successful in their lives, if they can make progress in their respective fields, reach to higher positions, and contribute to the society and the country, then the purpose of the book would be served.

—Medha Kirit

Acknowledgments

While writing this book many helped just because their love on Taai. Everyone's concern was that this book should reflect her personality in a proper way, so they made themselves available for 24×7 during this process. I don't want to thank them and get rid of them, but will be happy to remain in their obligations. This page is my gratitude towards them to enrich the content of this book.

Taai's daughter in Law–Snehal loved me a lot and supported me like her name– *Snehal*- Loving , Son Milinddada and grandson Siddhrath were reserved force for me as and when required.

My family Dr. Kirit, Son Neil, Daughter in Law Divya, My brother Dr. Kedar, Sisters Manjiri and Vrinda are my true back bones. They always bear with my tantrums and tried to keep my moral high. They all will be there with me for all my future ventures.

And all others who helped me in making this possible.

- Mr. Sunil Tated
- Mr. Sachin Chaturvedi
- Mr. Rama Dutt
- Mr. Harish Kashyap
- Mr. Pankaj Kshirsagar
- Smt. Rashmi Roy
- Smt. Jyoti Muzumdar

- Smt. Dr. Vatsala Joshi Pande
- Mr. Parakram Shekhavat
- Smt. Sharayu Waghmare
- Mr. Nagesh Namjoshi
- Mr. Arvind Javalekar
- Mr. Yogesh Vartak
- Smt. Vandana Mhaskar
- Mr. Krishna Upadhyay
- Mr. Rajesh Mishra
- Smt. Vrinda Shahasane
- Mr. Pankaj Bisht
- Smt. Seema Sayyad
- Smt. Uma Shah.
- Mr. Anand Limaye
- Mr. Chandrashekhar Kulkarni.
- Smt. Sharmila Bhagwat

Contents

1

Sumitra Mahajan Elected as Lok Sabha Speaker

दक्ष धूर्त योग्य तार्किक।
सत्य साहित्य नेमक भेदक।
कुशल चपल चमत्कारिक।
नाना प्रकारे॥

Daksha dhurta yogya tarkik.
Satya sahitya nemak bhedak.
Kushal chapal chamatkarik.
Nanaprakare.

(Dasbodh, 2.8.13)

(Extremely intelligent, multi-talented, wily, competent, logical Impartial, honest, litterateur, precise and penetrating, Skillful, agile and miraculous are the various amazing qualities).

—Samarth Ramdas

"Smt. Sumitra Mahajan is unanimously elected Speaker of the 16th Lok Sabha. I request her to come on the stage and accept the charge," declared the Pro-tem Speaker of the 16th Lok Sabha and senior-most MP in Parliament, Shri Kamal Nath. Everyone's attention turned towards Sumitrataai amidst a big round of applause.

Slowly, Smt. Sumitra Jayant Mahajan stood up. A mixed smile adorned her face – along with the happiness of achievement, there was a solemnity of a huge responsibility. The entire House gave a thunderous applause. She accepted greetings from all, including Prime Minister Shri Narendra Modi, veteran leaders Shri Lal Krishna Advani and Shri Mallikarjun Kharge. With a smile she strode on to the platform. Adjusting her 'pallu' carefully, as a habit, she smiled innocently, bent her head a bit and accepted the greetings from leaders of all parties with folded hands. She graced the chair when Pro-tem Speaker Shri Kamal Nath requested her to take the seat.

"I wholeheartedly thank the House and all of you," said Sumitrataai with a familiar smile.

When *Taai* laughs effortlessly, the empty space is visible in the upper arch in the right side of the mouth due to molar fall out. The hollowness simply adorns her round fair face; similar to the dark spot on the surface of the full moon, in the shape of a rabbit, just like a *nazar tika*.

Pro-tem Speaker of Lok Sabha: After a General Election, the Lok Sabha comes into existence. The leader of the political party which secures an absolute majority in the Lok Sabha is appointed as the Prime Minister of the country.

The Speaker and Deputy Speaker have the responsibility of running the Lok Sabha. The elected MPs appoint the Speaker. This election also requires a temporary Speaker. The Pro-tem Speaker of Lok Sabha is a temporary Speaker appointed for a limited period of time to conduct the works in the Lok Sabha after the General Elections. As per conventional practice, the senior-most MP is selected as a Pro-tem Speaker. The appointment has to be approved by the President. The

Pro-tem Speaker performs the duties of the office of the Speaker from the time of commencement of the sitting of the Lok Sabha till the election of the Speaker. However, once a new Speaker is elected, the Pro-tem Speaker ceases to function in the same capacity.

Veteran leader Shri Kamal Nath was appointed the Pro-tem Speaker to the 16th Lok Sabha. He had been elected nine times from the Chhindwara Lok Sabha constituency of Madhya Pradesh. Hon'ble President Shri Pranab Mukherjee appointed Shri Kamal Nath as Pro-tem Speaker in a simple ceremony. Vice President Shri Hamid Ansari, Prime Minister Shri Narendra Modi, Parliamentary Affairs Minister Shri Venkaiah Naidu and Parliamentary Affairs Minister of State Santosh Gangwar were present on the occasion.

The Pro-tem Speaker Shri Kamal Nath declared Smt. Sumitra Mahajan as an elected Speaker of the 16th Lok Sabha. She was the only MP elected eight consecutive times from Madhya Pradesh (the longest serving woman Member of Parliament). Taai was unanimously elected as the Speaker of the 16th Lok Sabha and thus became the second woman Speaker of Independent India. A pleased Shri Kamal Nath congratulated Prime Minister Shri Narendra Modi, by saying, "You have given justice to Madhya Pradesh."

Smt. Sumitra Jayant Mahajan, who is popularly known as *Taai,* basically is from Chiplun in Konkan region of Maharashtra. Her father Shri Purushottam Neelkanth Sathe alias Appa Sathe was a renowned lawyer in Chiplun. He was a great admirer of Marathi dramas and was Vibhag Sanghachalak of the Rashtriya Swayamsevak Sangh (RSS). Her mother Usha was a housewife, who took great interest in social work. After getting married to Advocate Jayant Mahajan on 29

January, 1965, Taai came to Indore. She was only 22-years old then. Her husband was a renowned lawyer. Sumitratai's in-laws wholeheartedly supported her in pursuing her education further. She earned her MA and LLB from Indore and also worked as a teacher for some time in a school run by an educational institute. Eventually she became a proud mother of two sons – Milind and Mandar.

Her in-laws were socially conscious and also actively participated in various social activities. *Taai* started delivering *pravachane* (religious discourses) and even doing social work along with her mother-in-law.

The first responsibility that came her way was during the Emergency. Helping and supporting the volunteers and their families who were imprisoned under the Maintenance of Internal Security Act (MISA), *Taai* travelled all over the city on her bicycle and later on the scooter throughout the day.

Then she was asked by the Bharatiya Janata Party (BJP) to actively work for the party and this marked her entry into politics. Sumitra Mahajan started her political career as an alderman -corporator in Indore Municipal Corporation in 1984. She was later elected as Deputy Mayor of Indore Municipal Corporation. She also contested the Indore Assembly elections but lost to Shri Mahesh Joshi. Thereafter, she won consecutively eight times from the Indore Lok Sabha constituency. In 2014, she was unanimously elected as the Speaker of the 16th Lok Sabha. Before her, Smt. Meira Kumar was the Speaker. Thus, Smt. Sumitra Mahajan became the second woman Speaker of independent India.

Previously she also served as Union Minister of State, holding the portfolios for Human Resource Development, Communications and Information Technology and Petroleum and Natural Gas. She had a vast experience in administrative work.

Taai says, "When I entered politics, people asked, 'Why

did you enter politics? It is so corrupt, so unethical!' My response was, 'How can we say that?' I tried to convince them by giving an example. 'Sitting on the bank of a river we cannot call the river dirty! We need to dive in the river to clean the dirt.' I entered politics with an ambition to do something good, something positive!"

After *Taai* assumed the office of Speaker, leaders of all political parties delivered speeches congratulating her. The speech by Prime Minister Shri Narendra Modi was quite significant as he said, "You are a public representative and have come here after facing all the challenges. You have been working in the society for many years – you have worked as an MP for eight consecutive terms and prior to that, worked in the Municipal Corporation twice. That is why you are well aware of people's problems and that would be beneficial for the house." He made a pun on her name and said, "Your name 'Sumitra' itself signifies making good friendship. Your behaviour is true to your name. This will be useful to run the House without any obstructions." While referring to her surname 'Mahajan', the Prime Minister remarked, "A *subhashit* in Sanskrit reads, '*Mahajano yen gatah sa panthah*' (The path by which great men go, that path is exemplary) and here 'Mahajan' has graced the seat to guide us. Thus Lok Sabha would definitely run smoothly, safely on the path shown by you."

There were a lot of expectations by all from *Taai*.

Responding to the congratulatory speeches and thanking all, she read out a speech penned by her. *Taai* said "I indeed feel honoured that you all have unanimously appointed me the Speaker; however, it is also a challenge for me. I am aware that there were a lot of anticipations from me when you congratulated me. I will try my best to fulfill all the hopes on the basis of my past experience of 25 years. I hope I will receive the cooperation from all in this endeavour. Parliament is a temple of democracy; it should witness a healthy discussion on public welfare. 66.48% voters have wholeheartedly voted for and elected us as representatives in Lok Sabha.

This Parliament cherishes a grand dream of creating a peaceful, progressive and contented society. I hope you all will support me in running the House uninterruptedly."

Taai also remembered her ideal Devi Ahilyabai as she said, "The intelligent and cultured MPs should abide by the glorious tradition of healthy discussion. They should remember that *rashtra sarvopari hai* (nation is paramount)."

Referring to Mr. Mavalankar, the first Speaker of Parliament, she saluted him. She respected the tradition and also stressed the need to introduce new practices with the help of the House. She thanked the Lok Sabha secretariat and everybody again. She quoted a Sanskrit *shloka* invoking the Almighty with dedication and servitude,

"Ajayam atmasamarthyam sushilam lok pujitam
dnyanam cha dehi vishvesh, dhyeya marga prakashakam."

The lines clearly reflected her emotions.

Taai was determined to ensure the proceedings were smoothly run in Lok Sabha. Thus, soon after becoming the Speaker, *Taai* minutely studied the background of all the MPs. She not only tried to understand the name and background of each MP, but gained information about the state, party, ideology, age, family, economic condition, education, hobby, etc. and accordingly categorised the classification – as IAS officials, educationists, doctors, economists, lawyers, defence persons, finance experts, scientists, etc. The Lok Sabha (Lower House of Parliament) had intellectuals and experts as its members. She noted the importance and usefulness of all. She studied minutely the responsibilities and powers of the Speaker and decided to adopt a working strategy for routine work and another for some periodical work so that the proceedings would be easily conducted.

Many television channels and journalists interviewed *Taai* on that day. As a study material for this writing, I saw nearly ten interviews given by *Taai* on that day. What was pleasantly surprising was that *Taai* had the same freshness, enthusiasm and serene smile in all the interviews. Many tried to cross-question her, corner her but she answered all the questions effortlessly, constantly seeking cooperation from the media and discretion of the journalists to help in bringing about rapid progress of the country.

Noted journalist Arnab Goswami asked a pointed question during the course of an interview, "Who would be appointed the leader of the Opposition?"

□

Hon'ble Lok Sabha Speaker Sumitrataai Mahajan	
https://youtu.be/7EQkcc9s4GQ	

Sumitra Mahajan elected Lok Sabha Speaker —Congratulations	
https://www.youtube.com/watch?v=vROqD4BeSVw	

2
Taking up the Responsibility

महायेत्ने सावधपणे।
समई धारिष्ट्य धरणे।
अद्भुतचि कार्य करणे।
देणे ईश्वराचे॥

Mahayetne savadhapane.
Samai dharishtya dharane.
Adbhutachi karya karane.
Dene ishvarache.

(Dasbodh, 18.6.15)

(To make sincere efforts with utmost concentration, to have courage when needed and to be able to fulfill outstanding tasks are gifts of God).

—Samarth Ramdas

The General Elections to the 16th Lok Sabha were held in nine phases, from 7 April to 12 May, 2014. The results were declared on May 16. The Bharatiya Janata Party-led National Democratic Alliance (NDA) scored an outright majority by winning 282 out of the total 543 seats. The situation of all the other parties was very precarious. The strength of the ruling party, the Congress, dropped down from 206 to 44. On May 26, Narendra Modi became the Prime Minister and along with him, some members were sworn in as ministers. Despite being a senior leader in the Lok Sabha, Smt. Sumitra Mahajan was not included as a minister. It was then assumed that the responsibility of the Lok Sabha would fall on *Taai's* shoulders. And *Taai* was unanimously elected as the Speaker of the Lok Sabha on 5 June, 2014.

"Who would be the leader of the Opposition?" asked noted journalist Arnab Goswami. Paying no heed to the question, *Taai* said, "I have taken charge just now, thus let me study the matter for a while. I will talk to experts on this subject; there are still three or four days to decide."

However, at the age of 72, *Taai's* life had changed drastically. *Taai*, who would rush to Indore whenever possible, would not be able to go there for several days now. Indore city was gearing up to welcome *Taai*. People were excited; the city was illuminated, firecrackers were burnt, sweets were distributed all over the city, while *Taai* was getting adjusted to her new responsibilities in Delhi.

Taai's schedule was becoming hectic. In fact, *Taai* had always lived a quiet and peaceful life, but it suddenly picked up momentum as soon as she was declared the Speaker.

Security guards all around, very busy schedule, many secretaries, assistants, several suggestions, countless visitors, a variety of people seeking appointments and some challenging matters to deal with! But *Taai* got adjusted to all and easily adapted herself to the new lifestyle. Her previous ministerial experience came in handy, though the new responsibility was quite different from the previous duty. Earlier the party was the first priority; now it was necessary to be impartial. The guidance of the veteran leaders was easily available. Now *Taai* was a veteran as she patiently listened to everyone. When required, she even sought guidance from experts. The issue of ego or prestige never came in her way. She believed in carrying out the assigned responsibilities to the best of her efforts. She took extra care that no one pointed a finger at her and always spoke with proper study and research.

When the Lok Sabha session was on, *Taai's* day would start a night before. The Lok Sabha office used to provide information on the proceedings and the issues that would crop up on the table next day. She studied the matters thoroughly, sometimes even till late night.

Next day, after getting up, she would exercise for some time and later discuss the day's events with her assistants. By then the assistants handling press and media would select some of the news for her to go through. Some of the clippings were then set aside for reference and reading. Then she would look at the files and sign, discuss all of them and prepare herself for the topics that can come up that day, decide on the MPs or the Ministers to be contacted for that and also to consult with the Parliamentary Affairs Minister. Then she would be ready to go to Parliament.

Sometimes she would attend functions or appointments before going to Parliament. Then the proceedings of Lok Sabha started. The first hour was question-answer session followed by zero hour. Many important questions came to the fore. Later some starred and un-starred questions were discussed.

After the lunch break, usually Deputy Speaker Thambi Duraiji or other senior member would take the seat. Although she was busy with other work, her attention was constantly focused on the Parliament proceedings shown on Lok Sabha Doordarshan. If the proceedings were to be slower than expected, "Today it will be 9 p.m.," she remarked. Then she would go to her chamber and complete the work. If she sensed some problem in some important discussion, then she would rush to Parliament House to control the situation. The work should go on smoothly – that was her only priority!

During the lunch break also, she had some important meetings lined up with national and international leaders.

Sometimes she would get annoyed as she never liked to talk, especially when she was eating or drinking tea. She preferred to focus on it. But usually it was impossible and she had to talk either to a person who came to meet her or with assistants or sometimes with the press.

But in any case, she was always the perfect host to her guests!

On holidays also she would go to the Parliament House for some work. Once, while *Taai* was in the Parliament House with her assistant, the headmaster of a government school in Haryana came to take the students on a round of the Parliament House. He was disappointed as it was a holiday. One of *Taai's* associate noticed it and prepared a pass to take everyone inside. But in all this mess, the work for which he had come, got delayed. *Taai* was waiting. She got angry and called the assistant. When she came to know of the mess created, she called all the children inside her office and chatted with them, while offering them cold drinks and snacks. The day became memorable for the headmaster and the students. *Taai* loved to talk to students and to show the Parliament House to the general public. She always said, "This is the temple of democracy and all citizens should see it."

The Members of Parliament are regarded important in the Lok Sabha as they are directly elected by the people and generally represent 10 to 20 lakh voters. The newly-elected members of the party are the MPs, who elect the leader of their party. The MPs from the party that wins the majority of seats elect its leader. The leader of the House becomes the Prime Minister. The MPs of the chief Opposition party elect their leader who becomes the leader of the Opposition. When time and need arises, the experienced leader of the Opposition is ready to form an alternative government. The work of the leader of the Opposition is not as difficult as that of a Prime Minister, but it is nevertheless important.

The Opposition is an essential part of a democratic government. Effective criticism is expected from the Opposition. The government rules create the system and implement the policies. The leader of the Opposition criticises. The main task of the leader of the Opposition is to make sure that the government is moving in the right direction. Thus the functions and rights of both the ruling party and the Opposition are important in a democracy.

It is true that the post of leader of the Opposition should be given to the leader of the party which comes second; however, the important point is that the party should have won at least 10 per cent of the seats.

The Speaker of the first Lok Sabha was Shri Ganesh Vasudeo alias G.V. Mavalankar. According to the rules laid down by the committee set up under the chairmanship of Mavalankar, a party which has secured at least 10 per cent seats would be eligible to become the main Opposition party at the national level and only a leader elected by the newly elected MPs of that party can become the leader of the Opposition. It is also alleged that as per the Protection of Human Rights Act 1993, Central Vigilance Commission Act 2003, Right to Information Act 2005, Lokpal and Lokayukta Act, 2013 and the National Judicial Appointments Commission Act, 2014, etc., the presence of the leader of the Opposition is required, but is not mandatory and this becomes a point of contention!

There may be several parties in the Opposition, but the main Opposition party is the second important party with a temporary minority. The Congress party, that lost power, was the main national Opposition party. However, at that time of the elections, the number of seats won by the party and the combined seats of some provincial parties were more. The big question was: Why did a political party desire to be recognised as the leader of the Opposition when there were not even 10 per cent MPs in the Parliament? Was it inevitable/

mandatory to have a leader of the Opposition in a democracy? In such a scenario, should the ruling government leave some seats for any party to choose a leader of the Opposition? Or the Mavalankar rule of securing at least 10 per cent seats to become the main Opposition party had become outdated? Should the Speaker approve the leader of the party who secured at least 10% of the total votes as the leader of the Opposition instead? Why did the ruling party not want an Opposition leader? Many such issues had cropped up.

The Mavalankar Rule

The 10 per cent rule was spelt out by G.V. Mavalankar, who was the first Lok Sabha Speaker. Mavalankar had ruled in the Lok Sabha that the strength of the main Opposition party, to be officially recognised as such, must be equal to the quorum of the House. The quorum is equivalent to 10 per cent of the members.

The statutory definition of the leader of Opposition, however, came with the salary and allowances of leader of Opposition Act of 1977. It said that the leader of the Opposition would be chosen from the Opposition party having the greatest numerical strength and recognised as such by the Lok Sabha Speaker or the Rajya Sabha Chairperson in the respective Houses.

The 1977 Act did not set the 10 per cent condition but Mavalankar's rule was a directive to the Speaker and was enforceable as law. This Mavalankar rule was finally incorporated in Direction 121(1) in Parliament (Facilities) Act 1998. This rule remains unchanged.

At the same time, it is true that a recognised Opposition leader is equal to a minister. He is provided with salary and gets many facilities, such as daily allowance, accommodation, travel allowance, medical treatment, telephone and secretariat facilities and vehicle facility.

When *Taai* became the Speaker, the first challenge she confronted was the election of the leader of the Opposition. *Taai's* first impression was that since the Congress was the second largest party, there was no harm in giving it the post. Basically *Taai* always believed in the politics of association and cooperation. When *Taai* contested the election, her main rival was late Prakash Chandra Sethi. They had never made any irresponsible statements against each other in the run-up to the elections. What is more the late Sethi's wife considered *Taai* as her fourth daughter. Considering *Taai's* nature, she did not find it wrong to give the position of the leader of the Opposition to the Congress.

But the post of the Lok Sabha Speaker is based on different rules. There is a tradition; there are footsteps laid by the predecessors. The Speaker of the Lok Sabha is bound by the framework.

During Pandit Nehru's tenure, from 1952 to 1969, no party was able to win even 10 per cent of the seats. There were Opposition leaders, like the late Syama Prasad Mookerjee, the late Ram Manohar Lohia, but no Opposition party had the required strength. So, no leader of the Opposition was appointed. So it happened that during Indira Gandhi's tenure and when Rajiv Gandhi became the Prime Minister, the place of the leader of the Opposition remained vacant due to this rule.

Evaluating the matter, *Taai* took the important decision that the then Congress leader, Mallikarjun Kharge could not become the leader of the Opposition. Thus Munisamy Thambidurai of the All India Anna Dravida Munnetra Kazhagam (AIDMK) and MP from Karur in Tamil Nadu was elected as the Deputy speaker.

Thus *Taai* began her career as the Speaker with the important lesson that 'the honour of the position and preserving the tradition and rules is more important than the idea and opinion of an individual.'

India did not have a leader of Opposition till 1969. In the first three Lok Sabha elections, the Congress-led by Pandit Jawaharlal Nehru had an overarching influence. Nehru's Congress party won the Lok Sabha elections in 1951-52, 1957 and 1962 with an overwhelming majority and the main Opposition parties consistently failed to win the requisite 10 per cent of the seats.

□

Celebrations	
https://youtu.be/xFvUSnpKALQ	

3
Welcome and Felicitation in Indore and Chiplun

लोकी लोक वाढविणे।
तेणे अमर्याद जाले।
भूमण्डळी सत्ता चाले।
गुप्तपणें॥

Loki loka vadhavine.
Tene amaryad jale.
Bhumandali satta chale.
Guptapane.

(Dasbhodh, 15.2.26)

(He is able to increase the number of people gathered around him beyond measure with his powers on Earth that work in hidden ways. People are attracted to him and he makes people work unitedly).

—Samarth Ramdas

Taai's birthplace is Chiplun and Indore is her *karmabhoomi* (workplace). Of course, there cannot be a comparison between a small town like Chiplun and the vibrant city of Indore with a glorious past. Hailing from a small city in Konkan, Sumitrataai not only adapted herself to the new life but being mild-mannered, she has, over the years, emerged as a force to reckon with in Indore where she has never lost any election since she first became an MP in 1989.

Invincible Sumitratai has ruled the hearts of the people like her ideals, Mother Jijabai and Ahilyabai. Not for few years, but for more than four decades! When she rose to the top post of the Lok Sabha as the Speaker, she became *Taai* of the people all over the country. In Marathi, *Taai* means elder sister, who takes care of others, like a mother. And true to the title, *Taai* has showered people with love and affection. She has considered their share of problems as her own and done whatever she could do to resolve the issues.

Before Sumitratai's rise in Indore politics, Indore was a stronghold of the Congress, but later the BJP snatched it from the Congress. *Taai* held the post of MP for 30 years and passed the reins of power on to her successor, the current BJP MP, Mr. Shankar Lalwani.

When *Taai* was unanimously elected the Speaker of Lok Sabha, the entire Indore wore a festive look. The people eagerly awaited her arrival. However, *Taai* could not come to Indore immediately. When she came to her hometown for the first time after becoming the Speaker, she was given a grand and rousing welcome. She visited Raj Wada area and garlanded the bust of Devi Ahilyabai Holkar. As the grand procession marched to the civic reception, the musical instruments, such as *dhol, tashe, vajantri chaughada* heralding her arrival, the activists greeted her with garlands at every square in the city. At the venue of the felicitation function, a large number of citizens eagerly awaited her arrival to greet her and listen to her speech.

A million memories flashed through Sumitrataai's mind. She remembered the days when she as Sumitra Purushottam Sathe married lawyer, Jayant Mahajan, and came to Indore. She never expected to get such respect, love and honour in her life. That is why she became quite emotional while replying to the felicitation.

Taai said, "I have been elected as the Speaker of the Lok Sabha; the seat of honour that has been offered to me is not mine but of the people of Indore." In a lighter vein, she added, "We are called Speaker but we are not supposed to speak much. The one who speaks the least is the best speaker." In an interview about people's love, her reply was that "love is from both sides. I came to politics from social work, to serve the people. I did it honestly and people loved me too." This was certainly evident at the time of public felicitation.

Sumitra Mahajan may have held a top constitutional post but her family remained her first priority. She is very sensitive and believed in building relations and taking people along. I have also witnessed an incident when Sumitratai was a Minister of State in Prime Minister Atal Bihari Vajpayeeji's cabinet. Kiritji Somaiya (my husband) received a phone call to gather information about 'Mauli' Old Age Home in Borwadi that *Taai* wanted to visit. Luckily my uncle Aaba Oak was the main trustee there. Naturally, the responsibility of taking *Taai* to the old age home fell on me. *Taai's* aunt was disabled and had no children; that is why she came to 'Mauli' during the last stage of her life. She wished to meet Sumitrataai. An old woman who lived with *Taai's* aunt sent an ordinary postcard expressing the desire of *Taai's* aunt. *Taai* had no idea about the condition of her aunt. As soon as she received the postcard, she decided to meet her aunt. Sumitrataai came to the small village with all her siblings and spent one full day with her aunt. *Taai* always cared for emotional bonding.

Rashtra Sevika Samiti, had organised a felicitation programme at Jijamata Bhavan in Thane, near Mumbai. All the members were delighted that a *sevika* had become the Speaker of Lok Sabha. *Sevikas* from all over Mumbai and nearby areas had gathered to greet *Taai*. The auditorium was fully packed.

A big screen was arranged in an adjacent room (hall). The programme was a huge success. *Taai* came to the hall where the screen was arranged. "The *sevikas* had come out of love. *Sevikas* in the adjacent room could not see me personally; how can I leave without meeting them all?" *Taai* said. Before leaving the venue, she made sure she met all the *sevikas*. This genuine care, affection and warmth makes *Taai* unique.

At the time of felicitation in Indore, Sumitrataai particularly remembered her in-laws and she also mentioned them in her speech. She said, "Indore gave us everything. We came from an ordinary family. We were happy wherever we went and were satisfied with what we got. My father-in-law's grandmother came to Mumbai from Konkan with two small children, after the death of her husband. She struggled to make the two ends meet. There she met friends who were originally from Konkan and settled in Indore. With their encouragement, the grandmother came to Indore and started earning a living for herself and her children. One of her sons became a school teacher and later, the headmaster, while the other started his own saree-dyeing factory. He was the father of my father-in-law. When he started the factory, he worked with the principle to hire only needy women to help them and pay off *matru rina* (mother's debt). Gradually hosiery clothes, such as sweaters, mufflers, socks, etc. came to be manufactured in the factory. When I got married, my father-in-law ran the factory. I still remember that he always distributed the first lot of clothes in the factory among the poor."

Taai Talks about the Mahajan Family

...Kashinath Mahajan lived at Kelshi, in Maharashtra. He had two sons– the eldest was Hari and the youngest one was Sakharam. Kashinath Pant died when the children were five or six years old. After his death, his wife and children faced troubles in the house. Tired of

the family bickering, the widow left her home one night with her two children. Somehow she reached Mumbai. She earned her living by working as a cook and midwife. Luckily she met a family (I think their surname was Ketkar) from Indore. She came to Indore with them assuring all help. She was a grandmother of my father-in-law. She had to face difficulties at every stage in her life but undaunted, she continued to toil for the sake of her children. Tall, disciplined and dignified lady, she took every care to give good education to her children. The elder son, Haripant was a teacher and later became the headmaster of a school. The younger son, Sakharampant started his own business of saree dyeing. He later turned to manufacture of hosiery clothes, such as sweaters, cotton socks, mufflers, etc. The socks were supplied to the military. Sakharampant had witnessed his mother's suffering and struggle. Thus, he strictly followed a rule to employ needy women in his factory. Many women used to take home the work of knitting and buttoning sweaters. Even I had seen all this after my marriage and even learnt to knit toes of socks! Gradually, the two brothers built a house in Nandalalpur. Both the brothers got married. Sakharampant had two children– the first child was a girl and after two or three years, a boy (my father-in-law) Vaman Sakharam, was born. But before he was a year old, his mother, Sakharampant's wife, died. Haripant did not have any children. But both the children were raised with love by Haripant's wife. She worked hard to stitch socks, etc. Later she could not see properly or even walk due to old age. I have seen my mother-in-law caring and nursing her. Sometimes, even I helped her. My father-in-law's father passed away when he was 19-20 years old. Later my father-in-law developed the hosiery business. Haripant was very disciplined and loved all his grandchildren– Jayant, Vasant and Hemant. However, my husband Jayantrao was his favourite. My in-laws respected and adored Haripant. My father-in-law also appreciated his grandmother very much and have heard many interesting stories about her from him.

"Thus, Indore has given us a lot. It taught us honesty and philanthropy; gave us stability and respect.

I am fully aware that this congratulatory letter that you have given me today is not a letter of appreciation but a letter of expectation. I will do my best to meet the expectations, to be trustworthy. With your love and encouragement, I will do my best to fulfill the responsibility given to me, make all of you proud by serving all the people in the country," *Taai* announced. It was Kushabhau Thakre who encouraged Taai to enter politics. *Taai* had an urge to pursue her education after marriage. She wanted to become financially independent. Her in-laws were very supportive. She started learning further and began to participate in literary meets and women's organisations. Around the same time, she came in contact with Mrs. Mainatai Gokhale, a preacher (*pravachankar*) from Indore. She also started giving *pravachane* (*kirtans*) herself on the *Ramayana*. *Taai* was interested in social work since childhood and gradually joined the Rashtra Sevika Samiti. She also started teaching in a school for homeless and adult women, run by a social organisation called Saraswati Mahila Shikshan Sangh.

At the time of Emergency, the Rashtriya Swayamsevak Sangh and affiliated organisations started helping the affected families. *Taai's* mother-in-law had full faith in her daughter-in-law and appreciated her and gave her full support. Her entry into politics was quite sudden. She just knew that she had to do RSS work. The idea of joining politics was discussed at home. She had been married for 12-15 years by now. Her husband Jayantrao gave her the freedom to do whatever she wanted to do after taking good care of the home. *Taai* became a member of the Municipal Council on behalf of the BJP. With the energy of *sanskars* acquired from her mother and the encouragement of her in-laws, *Taai* was all set to fly high.

When *Taai* became the Lok Sabha Speaker, there were celebrations and jubilations not only in Indore and Madhya Pradesh, but also in Chiplun and Konkan. Large flex boards were erected all around Konkan. Several days after becoming the Speaker of Lok Sabha, *Taai* got an opportunity to visit her native place, Chiplun. The excitement and enthusiasm of the villagers knew no bounds. Entire Chiplun wore a festive look. The BJP and Shiv Sena were in alliance then. MP Shri Anant Geete, BJP leader Dr. Vinay Natu, and others had arranged a two-day grand programme to greet *Taai*. "As the village became visible from the plane, I remembered the lines by V.B. Pathak: "*Kuna gavachya disu lagalya spashta mala lochani ude kiti khalbal mazya hridayatuni*"."

(Now that the signs of native place are clearly visible, Oh, what a turmoil and elation it stirs in my heart!) My condition was exactly the same."

Taai is very fond of literature. No matter how busy she is, she makes it a point to read newspaper supplements, poems, short stories, novels and other literary works. She keeps aside newspaper clippings for reference. She knows many poems, lyrics, *stotras* by heart. Kusumagraj is her favourite poet and her favourite poem is *Prithviche Prem Geet*. *Taai* has inherited her love for literature from her father.

After a warm welcome in Chiplun, *Taai* visited Kanya Shala, a school where she studied from Standard I to VII. The girls at the school flocked to see *Taai*. Keeping aside all the protocols and security rules, *Taai* freely mingled with the villagers and friends. After visiting the village deity Ganpati Mandir and Lakshmi Narayan Mandir, she walked through the

Bendurkar Aali where she had lived before marriage. She met her old friends. One of her friends informed us, "*Taai* studied in 'Kanya Shala' up to 7th standard and then studied in United English School till 11th standard. She passed her 11th class in 1959/60. But in December, her father died and she shifted to Mumbai to study. But she never forgot us and kept in touch with us through her letters. Our friendship has continued even after so many years." *Taai* appreciated the efforts of one of her friends, Saroj Nene, who had nicely arranged the newspaper clippings on *Taai* in a notebook. *Taai* chatted freely with everyone, had a hearty laugh and revived her precious memories.

The visit could not have been completed without visiting Lord Parashurama. At the grand reception that followed, *Taai* expressed her feelings, "Chiplun shaped us. It nurtured us. We really grew up as the children of the village. The village supported us. It gave us strength to face any challenge in life. We used to gather at the grounds of Laxmi Narayan Mandir for the Samiti Shakha. We attended many lectures and also heard that my father's lectures were also held here.

"The felicitation function that has been organised is a very special one because Chiplun is not my area of political work. You are not my voters. You have no expectations from me. However, you are happy that I have become the Speaker of Lok Sabha. The love and appreciation offered to me is an unconditional compliment to a *mahervashini* (who has her maternal home here) and that is why it is special."

Taai further said, "The first Speaker of the Lok Sabha, Mr. Mavalankar was also from Ratnagiri in Konkan. He worked honestly and impartially and gave honour to the post of the Speaker. I assure you that I will also work similarly."

Later, when *Taai's* school friends visited Delhi, she welcomed them with love and affection. She personally took them around the Parliament House and had a warm interaction with each of them. Even her friends felt proud of their friend Sumitraji, who, despite reaching the top post of Lok Sabha as Speaker, spared time to attend to them. Chiplun has always remained a special place for *Taai.* She and her siblings have made generous donations to the Lokmanya Tilak Library besides providing provided government grants to it.

Taai earned love and respect at Indore as well as at Chiplun and both the places are dear to her. She has been an unceasing link between Konkan and Malwa.

Once, on the day of Gudi Padva, at the Maharashtra Bhawan in Delhi, a Gudi erection programme at the hands of Taai, was organised. Here *Taai* remarked, "Today we are erecting a *Gudi* of power, strength and success." Then a journalist sarcastically asked her, "Are you from Chiplun or Indore? From Maharashtra or Madhya Pradesh?" She replied, "We follow the tradition of erecting Gudi in Indore also. We gather at the palace early morning, publicly erect a Gudi and distribute the *prasad* of coriander and jaggery. I am a daughter of Chiplun but a daughter-in-law of Indore." She further added with a smile, "Do you know that a daughter is that light placed on the threshold that lights up not only the house and also the courtyard; she illuminates, enlightens both her *maika* (bride's maternal home) as well as *sasural* (home of in-laws)."

□

<table>
<tr><td>Introduction of hon'ble Sumitrataai Mahajan</td><td rowspan="2"></td></tr>
<tr><td>https://speakerloksabha.nic.in/former/sumitra.asp</td></tr>
</table>

4

Managing the Responsibility of Speaker

सारासार विचार करणे।
न्याये अन्याये अखंड पाहणे।
बुद्धी भगवंताचे देणे।
पालटेना॥

Sarasar vichar karane.
Nyaye anyaye akhanda pahane.
Buddhi bhagawantache dene.
Palatena.

(Dasbodh, 10.8.29)

(One who appreciates and adopts the best qualities of sound judgement by going to the root of the problem and studying its pros and cons impartially, thoughtfully and through intelligent discernment– such qualities are a gift from God).

—Samarth Ramdas

"Now I am all for the country, belong to the country," *Taai* would say every Monday morning when she landed at Delhi airport. *Taai* would never leave Delhi when the Parliament session was on. Otherwise, she would fly to Indore on Friday evening and return to Delhi on Monday morning. As soon as she entered her car, she would start gathering all information from her assistant. The entire week's schedule was conveyed to her. Of course, it changed as required though most of it was planned. She would go through the necessary papers, also write remarks on them or sometimes make suggestions, etc. The list of works from Indore was also included. *Taai* never wasted a minute nor wasted any paper unnecessarily. She did not take a day off, but efficiently handled all the responsibilities given to her.

India's first Prime Minister, Pandit Jawaharlal Nehru had said, "In a parliamentary democracy, the Speaker represents the dignity and independence of the House and the House represents the country. Hence the Speaker of the Lok Sabha, in a way, becomes the symbol of a country's autonomy and independence."

Somnath Chatterjee was an influential Speaker in the country. *Taai* held great respect for him; he was like an elder brother to *Taai*. When she became the Speaker, she went to meet him at his house in Delhi and also went to Kolkata to pay her last respects when he died.

Taai says, "Somnath Dada was like an elder brother. I learned two important things from him. The first one is that the position we hold is supreme. After our decision, no one can appeal in the court. So we have to maintain the dignity of the position. The second one is that we should live up to our image and never cross our limits. If I ever went to the well of the House (the area immediately facing the Speaker) by mistake, he would immediately pull me up, 'Such things are not expected from you'."I followed his advice. And this is what I suggested to many women MPs also. Speak softly but firmly, rather than shouting to prove a point. I'm going to give everyone a chance to speak. Misconceptions, superficial knowledge would not work; a thorough study is important."When *Taai* became the

Speaker of the Lok Sabha, first of all she thoroughly studied the responsibilities of the post. Actually, she had known most of her tasks as she had been an MP since 1989, but she studied them minutely after becoming the Speaker. Under the Constitution, the Speaker occupies a prestigious position. In the House, the Prime Minister and all the ministers sit a little lower, while the Speaker of the Lok Sabha sits on the dais – '*vyasotcchishtam jagat sarvam*' and in order to carry out the duties in the name of such a great personality (*Vyas*), one has to be more vigilant. According to constitutional etiquette, the Speaker of the Lok Sabha occupies a very high position.

The Speaker's prime responsibility is to ensure smooth functioning of the Lok Sabha proceedings and the office of the Speaker has sufficient powers to assist him/her in the smooth functioning of Parliament. In the Lok Sabha chamber, the Speaker's chair is distinctively placed so that the Speaker gets a commanding view of the entire House from her chair. In front of them, the General Secretary of the Lok Sabha Secretariat and senior officials of the Secretariat sit at a semi-circular table and assist the Speaker in the conduct of parliamentary functions, dealings and proceedings. The Speaker has a staff of 5,200 employees.

According to the Indian Constitution, the Speaker has immense powers– both administrative and discretionary – which include the power to qualify or disqualify members. It is up to him/her to decide whether to allow an MP to speak or not. Sumitrataai was fully aware of this as well as the nature and behaviour of the MPs.

'Kamal Sakhi Manch' is an open platform for the wives of BJP MPs. A get-together was organised in each of the conventions. The practice had been continuing since 2009. An executive committee was formed under the guidance of Sumitrataai, Sushma Swaraj and Kamla Advani. All of them met at each other's house on the basis of rotation. They came together, exchanged ideas with each other and shared distinctive work carried out in particular areas. They also got some new insights about the work in their respective husbands' constituencies. The original idea was that only the wives of the MP's should be present at the event, but often the host invited an MP and his wife. When *Taai* organised the event, she did it in her own style. She maintained, "If I call MPs, then I will not be able to talk to the wives of MPs openly. I want to talk to them; I want to get to know them." On that day, *Taai* hosted the get-together in Malwa style. Everything from *rangoli* to '*paan'* was done in Malwa style; even the vegetables and cooks were called from Indore.

Taai always conducted every task, be it small or big, in her own distinctive style. Innovative ideas, proper homework, proficiency, quality of work, informal communication, full use of provisions and anticipation of upcoming issues or problems were some of the features of *Taai's* work. No wonder the work turned out to be perfect. *Taai* applied the same formula during her tenure as the Speaker.

Suresh Prabhu has been *Taai's* time–honoured colleague and family friend. When he came to know that I was writing on *Taai*, he began to talk animatedly about *Taai* and revealed many aspects of her personality. He said, "In 1996, when Hon'ble Atalji became the Prime Minister, I became an MP for the first time. I was included in the 13-day-Cabinet. Soon afterwards, the Atalji's government had to sit in the Opposition. *Taai* was dauntless but very kind and caring. She always tried to convince others about her point of view. She was never harsh, nor unfair. *Taai* was aggressive but at no time was she oppressive. I had witnessed this quality then. After a few years, the BJP government returned to power.

As the senior-most MP, *Taai*, became a minister. Our acquaintance developed further when she became the Minister of State for Human Resources.

The two responsibilities were totally different. The work of the Opposition is to evaluate and criticise the decisions of the ruling party which has to bear the brunt of the criticism by the Opposition and check the vociferous outbreaks with counter arguments. During that period, I would observe how *Taai* worked persistently within the limitations of the government. We lost power in 2004 and had to sit on the Opposition benches. We started working together and came to see another aspect of Sumitra Taai's distinctive personality. She accepted every change in her life easily and elegantly – first as a daughter, then as a housewife, then as an MP in the Opposition, then as a minister, and then again as leader of the Opposition. Sumitrataai was quite experienced by then and could work in all kinds of situations. In 2014 we saw her in yet another role.

Suresh Prabhu, the then Railway Minister said about her, "A unique responsibility came her way in 2014. She sat at the highest position as Speaker in the Lok Sabha. I can say without exaggeration that when she sat there, she enhanced the dignity of the position. When I was Railway Minister, I had to visit both the Houses. The Lok Sabha functioned quite smoothly and the Rajya Sabha did not function at all. Ananth Kumar used to say, 'The one and only reason is *Taai*'." Everything runs smoothly because of *Taai's* way of working– taking everyone along, her way of dealing with criticism of the Opposition, their behaviour– *Taai* has managed everything very well. There are problems, there are limitations; the government cannot be criticised. The public has many issues. People have to be faced. You have to work as a representative of the people even when you are the Speaker. *Taai* brilliantly maintained the balance, " Suresh Prabhu stated.

As Speaker of the Lok Sabha, she had to hold key positions of many committees:

Chairperson, (i) Business Advisory Committee (ii) Rules Committee (iii) Joint Parliamentary Committee on Maintenance of Heritage Character and Development of Parliament House Complex, (iv) Committee on Installation of Portraits/Statues of National Leaders and Parliamentarians in Parliament House Complex, (v) General Purposes Committee, (vi) Committee on Security in Parliament House Complex, (vii) Standing Committee of All India Presiding Officers' Conference; and (viii) Executive Committee of CPA India Region.

President, (i) Indian Parliamentary Group; and (ii) India Branch of the Commonwealth Parliamentary Association (CPA).

Concerned and Compassionate

In fact, *Taai* efficiently handled many positions at the same time. A gentle smile and affinity to all – are special characteristics of *Taai*. Whether they were associate MPs, assistants or Class IV employees, she paid serious attention to the day-to-day affairs of all of them because she knew very well that the employees would work more sincerely if they and their families were kept satisfied.

An employee was quite intelligent but he had some special problem because of which he was not sent out of the country for any training or government work. Taai was sharp enough to notice the fact, so she enquired the reason for this. When she learnt that he was not sent out because he was physically handicapped, she scolded the concerned officers and gave a letter of recommendation to the employee to visit abroad for work.

She did various welfare work for the officers and staff of the Lok Sabha Secretariat. These included important decisions related to promotion, training, cadre review, establishment of Joint Parliamentary Pay Committee, Annual Health Examination, etc. of the Secretariat staff. The implementation of these decisions, which had been pending for years, brought in unprecedented benefits for the officers and staff of the Secretariat. She also made arrangement for a space to set up a crèche for young children of the female staff of the Secretariat.

She was content to share the joys and sorrows of the working staff and to provide them with the necessary guidance and help, especially the Class IV employees. She would call everyone by their names. When she realised that the employees did not have good houses to stay and that the work of housing project was being delayed, she personally looked into the matter and speedily got 185 flats completed with well-equipped and state-of-the-art amenities in the ongoing residential complex in RK Puram area and handed it over in 2015. The staff of the Secretariat went to stay there. She gave special attention to ensure that all employees received special allowances during the convention. She quietly listened to the complaints of the employees and if possible, she would immediately contact the concerned officer and take remedial action. Not only this, *Taai* would call the officer on the scheduled date, to check if follow up action had been taken or not. She would offer monetary help to the needy and tell him to return it whenever possible. Even today, she receives many letters of well-being from her staff because she genuinely cared for her subordinates as the head of a family. *Taai* never considered 'an individual as unit' but always regarded 'a family as a unit'.

Late Ananth Kumar, the then Parliamentary Affairs Minister, was like a son to Taai. Jyoti Mazumdar, who worked with Taai, shares a touching incident, "On 27 October, 2018, Taai returned to Delhi from Bhopal around 8 p.m. While having dinner, Taai received a call from Tejasvini, Ananth Kumar's wife, who said, "Ananth Kumar is suffering from cancer. He is refusing to take any treatment. He thinks that his end time has come. Taai, if you were to come and explain, he will probably agree to go in for treatment." Taai was scheduled to fly to Argentina the next day at 3 p.m., that is, on the 28th to attend the meeting of G-20. Ananth Kumar was at his home in Bangalore. Taai decided to go to Bangalore. She consulted Amit Shah and Rajnath Singh.

She changed her programme overnight. She called Tejaswini and told her not to worry and assured her that she would visit her the next day. She asked her colleague, Sunil Tated, to change her schedule. On 28th, she flew to Bangalore by the 8:30 flight in the morning, met Ananth Kumar and Tejaswini and explained to him the need for treatment. She returned to Delhi at about 8.30 p.m. She then took the flight to Argentina the next morning on October 29 to fulfill her responsibility.

Taai was 76-years old, but she considered it imperative to meet Ananth Kumar and Tejaswini out of affection. However, Ananth Kumar could not survive the illness. Taai missed him very much in the remaining tenure.

Her Working Style

In Taai's office Ctrl+C and Ctrl+V were on Ctrl +X mode.

Taai could understand Copy and Paste posts immediately and would delete the posts instantly. Her associates, such as Sunilji Tated, Rama Dutt, Sachin Chaturvedi and Rajesh Mishra, had worked with her earlier. They were quite familiar with *Taai's* nature and temperament.

The person working with *Taai* needed to follow three principles:

1. Not to lie.
2. Not to assume anything.
3. Not to talk unnecessarily.

One who failed to follow these principles had to face *Taai's* ire. Her assistants used to joke, "*Nazar hati, durghatna ghati*!"

(Lose focus, calamity befalls!)

Taai maintained cordial relations with everyone– this genuine bond of unconditional love is maintained even today. Sometimes she would up at her colleague Rama Dutt's house and ask, "What has *Bhabhiji* made today? I am coming." *Taai* simply enjoys *dahi wade* but sweets are her favourite. She loves to eat any dessert and enjoys to talk on recipes. She loves to cook. *Taai* often carried a box of homemade sweets while visiting someone and would be quite satisfied if the dish was appreciated.

She had full faith in 'NEED TO KNOW' and speaking only what is essential.

Once, as the Speaker, she went to Indonesia for a meeting of the International Parliamentary Union. One of the topics of discussion was 'Parliamentary Security'. "Why should one discuss minute details about security system in the country? We should make a note of good points that are adopted by others," was her argument. .

Taai was quite concerned about the security of Parliament House. An Internal Security Committee was constituted. It had its closed-door meetings. It was ensured that not a single word of it was leaked outside. *Taai* was kept acquainted with new security measures and equipment. Drones, CCTV and a number of up-to-date security devices were installed in Parliament at her suggestions. Very often thick envelopes containing confidential information came from Intelligence Bureau, but she would open them all by herself, study them, write comments, and sent them back after sealing them properly. It was not noticed by any of the staff. Though this was part of the rules, *Taai* observed these quite religiously.

During her tenure, *Taai* undertook various measures to protect the Parliament House complex. Parliament House is a heritage building. Extensive works for its conservation and repair were carried out during her period. Adequate provision of 120 MW solar panels for energy conservation in the Parliament building complex, LED lighting in the campus, Wi-Fi facility and rain-water harvesting, was made in the campus. Under her supervision, the work of Parliament House Annexe, another building adjoining the Parliament House complex, was completed. Apart from office rooms, well-equipped committee rooms and halls were constructed. The building has been made environmentally friendly, perfect and safe.

The expansion work of the Western Court Hostel was also carried out. The building housed 82 additional rooms and today the building is well equipped with gym, yoga room, dining area, etc. The construction of these additional rooms has reduced the current and former MPs' expenditure on private hotels and saved government money. Under *Taai's* supervision, the construction of these rooms was completed six months before its scheduled date.

According to *Taai*, the Parliament House was the temple of democracy and the home of the people, and *Taai*, its chief caretaker. She considered it her duty to ensure its overall development. She also paid more attention to the infrastructure and qualitative development.

When *Taai* realised that about 300 MPs had been elected for the first time for the 16th Lok Sabha, she decided to train them properly. She carried out activities, such as explaining the rules, traditions, resolving their doubts and imparting guidance from experts, etc. Under the programme 'Dialogue with MPs' she held informal meetings with the newly-elected MPs and tried to understand their thoughts and wishes and shared her experiences with them.

Of course, *Taai* admonished those members who did not follow the rules. She had to deal with improper behaviour of members, such as breaking the tradition, entering the well, speaking unconstitutional language and behaviour, tearing papers, throwing pieces of papers, etc. Then *Taai* would get angry and agonised. She even expelled some members for their unruly behaviour a few times, but before reprimanding them, she would say, "I am sorry! I am sorry!" She felt very bad while doing all this. The conduct of the members is witnessed by the common man. The members were capable and that is why the people had elected them. Hence, it was her natural expectation that they should act responsibly. She felt that there should be discussion, there should be debate, ideological clashes, effective laws should be made and there should be public welfare work.

During her tenure of five years, she was witness to some unpleasant incidents which saddened her but she confronted them courageously. Arvind Kejriwal's AAP party opposed the improvements suggested by the Central Government in the Land Acquisition Act 2013. He said that the modifications were against the farmers. A big congregation of farmers gathered to protest against the Act at Jantar Mantar in New Delhi. The Congress party backed him. As the speeches continued, Gajendra Singh, a young man from Dausa village in Rajasthan, tied a rope to the tree with his own hands and committed suicide by hanging. The live telecast of the shocking incident was watched by the whole country. It was natural to see its wrong repercussions in all the four pillars of democracy. In a strong democracy, everyone is expected to recognise their responsibilities and behave properly, but unfortunately, this did not happen. Worst of all, there was a kind of a competition, a tug of war of blaming each other by all the parties. The Opposition groups called for repeal of the Bill and demanded discussion in the Lok Sabha. *Taai* agreed to it.

But the politicians and political parties were busy studying how this incident would help them fetch the maximum number of votes. Someone declared this youth a martyr; someone else put forth a resolution to erect a statue of him, while someone else criticised the act as anti-farmers. Whose fault was it – the Delhi Government's or the Central Government's and who was the saviour of the farmers? In other words, there was an uproar over who was the champion of the poor?

Even in the Lok Sabha, MPs from all parties were engaged in this game for two days. *Taai* had to be very patient in this difficult situation. A newspaper wrote, "Only *Taai* behaved thoughtfully." She repeatedly expressed her sadness over the incident and maintained that the issue of land acquisition could be resolved through discussions. *Taai* insisted on holding a healthy discussion wherein everyone would get a chance to speak and where everyone should speak. Even though there was a commotion in the House, she gave everyone a chance to speak. She managed the situation skilfully and sometimes even scolded them; at times, she spoke gently, especially when introducing the rules to the MPs and appealing for their cooperation. *Taai* repeatedly maintained that the farmers' issue is quite serious and a temporary solution is of no use; it is not proper also. Taai clearly opined that in order to prevent farmers' suicides, all the parties should try to find a solution with the help of experts.

Corruption in the Rafael fighter jet deal was another challenging issue during *Taai's* tenure. The Congress party had launched an aggressive campaign before the 2019 Lok Sabha elections, alleging corruption in the purchase of 36 Rafale fighter jets from France.

The apex court on 15 November, 2019, after giving a clean chit to the Modi government, said that there was no reason for the Central Bureau of Investigation (CBI) to lodge an FIR or a mobile inquiry into allegations of irregularities in the multi-billion-dollar transaction. In this case also, *Taai's* sober and restrained role as Speaker of the Lok Sabha was lauded.

Demonetisation

Demonetisation was another stormy issue to crop up during *Taai's* tenure. Both the Lok Sabha and Rajya Sabha could not function for some time. As Speaker of Lok Sabha, she had to face the criticism from the Opposition parties. At times it was quite frustrating also. The pros and cons of demonetisation is a different issue, but here it is essential to state her opinion on the subject. She looked at it as a part of a campaign against black money and corruption.

Hon'ble Prime Minister Shri Narendra Modiji mentioned five points while explaining the reason for such a step – curbing black money, banning counterfeit notes, removing corruption, controlling terrorism and Naxalism and give direct benefit to workers.

Lok Sabha Speaker Sumitra Mahajan reiterated the same points that demonetisation of old Rs. 500 and Rs. 1000 currency was a pre-planned, especially in view of the steps initiated by the Narendra Modi government, like the drive to open new Jan-Dhan accounts and facilitate direct benefit transfer. She asserted, "It is being said in discussions that the decision to demonetise currency notes was taken all of a sudden. But, if we look at the chain of events, then it seems that the government had planned it long back."

She said that the Centre was emphasising on opening bank accounts of all the countrymen under Jan-Dhan scheme since long. The government was also saying that wages under the Mahatma Gandhi National Rural Employment Guarantee Scheme would be deposited directly into the bank accounts.

"All these moves indicated that the government was considering reduction in the use of currency notes and pushing forward provisions of digital economy," she clarified. While sharing her personal conversation with Narendra Modi, *Taai* said the Prime Minister had recently told her that he wanted an arrangement wherein someone after having a '*paan*' (betel leaf) from a shop at a square could pay through a digital transaction.

She added that the PM had told her that this could be a possibility if some efforts were made in this direction. The black money could easily be identified by increasing the use of digital transactions. Besides, there would be no scope for bungling in the financial assistance given to beneficiaries of government schemes, she said.

Regional Parties and Central Government

The detailed discussion on the no-confidence motion tabled by the Telugu Desham Party has been discussed in a separate chapter, but at that time, the relationship between the regional parties and the ruling dispensation and the equation between the regional governments and the Central Government had come to the fore. However, its origins date back to the structuring of provinces based on language. Discussions were held with *Taai* on a number of issues, including the emergence of regional parties, their formation, their individual practices, their role in numerical electoral politics and their impact on national unity. *Taai* opines, "Everyone would think according to their regional priorities, but they should give first priority to the interests of the country."

Connected with Commoners

Taai always believed in interacting with the masses and maintaining a dialogue with them so as to bring the Parliament closer to the common masses. She felt that the general public, especially students and teachers from schools, colleges and educational institutions should get a chance to visit Parliament House to get a better understanding of Parliament and the democratic practices. What she enjoyed most was communicating with students who came from far off places and presenting them with small gifts, especially books which inculcated high values. This gave her immense pleasure and satisfaction in the midst of hectic Parliament proceedings.

Around 5 lakh people visited the premises of Parliament House, which is the highest temple of democracy, during the 16th Lok Sabha.

Reverence for Atalji

Taai venerated Hon'ble Atal Bihari Vajpayee and felt highly honoured to head the committee appointed to install a full-size oil painting of his in the Central Hall of Parliament House. She says, "When I was elected for the first time as the new MP, Atalji was our role model. His personality was larger than life. It would not be wrong to say that he taught us to walk by holding our hands."A full-length oil painting of Atal Bihari Vajpayee, the shining star of Indian politics and the most well-known former non-Congress Prime Minister, was unveiled by Hon'ble President Ram Nath Kovind. Hon'ble Atalji was an ideal; not a person. Anyone who comes to visit the Parliament House and stands in front of this oil painting will surely be impressed and inspired by Atalji's personality and work." That's what *Taai* said on the occasion.

No.	Subject	Presented	Result
1.	No-confidence motion	1	Rejected by voice vote after 11 hours of discussion
2.	Calling attention	18	Statements on it: 659
3.	General questions	6,460	Oral answers: 1,178
4.	Starred questions	6,244	4,718 answers
5.	Unstarred questions	73,405	Written answers given

6.	Bills	219 (govt.)	205 passed
7.	Constitutional Amendments	3	101- Goods and Services Tax (GST) 102- Aadhaar services and concessions 103- reservation for economically weaker groups in higher education
8.	Under Article 199	33	
9.	Suggestions by the Standing Committee	730	
10.	Adjournment motion Motion of no confidence	1	Rejected by voice vote after 11 hours of discussion
11.	Taai's speeches outside Lok Sabha	190	
12.	Duration of sessions	331 days	Worked for 1,190 hours out of a total of 1,612 hours Interruptions: 422 hours

Taai's Valedictory Speech

Speaker Sumitra Mahajan expressed her satisfaction over the performance of the 16th Lok Sabha when it came to an end on the last day of the Budget Session, that is, on 13 February, 2019. The House passed 205 out of the 219 Bills introduced during the entire period.

In her valedictory speech, she said that in the last five years since June 2014, the House had a total of 331 sittings of 1,612 hours, out of which 422 hours went in vain due to disruptions.

"She said the major legislations passed in the Lok Sabha include black money (undisclosed foreign income and assets) and Imposition of Tax Bill, 2015; Juvenile Justice (Care and Protection of Children) Bill, 2015; Insolvency and Bankruptcy Code, 2016; Benami Transactions (Prohibition) Amendment

Bill, 2016; Constitution (One Hundred and First Amendment) Bill, 2016 regarding introduction of the Goods and Services Tax."

The other Bills included Integrated Goods and Services Tax Bill, 2017; Aadhaar (Targeted Delivery of Financial and Other Subsidies, Benefits and Services) Bill, 2016; Mental Healthcare Bill, 2017; Constitution (One Hundred and Second Amendment) Bill, 2018 regarding constitution of the National Commission for Backward Classes under the newly inserted Article 338 B of the Constitution; Fugitive Economic Offender Bill, 2018; Scheduled Castes and the Scheduled Tribes (Prevention of Atrocities) Amendment Bill, 2018 and the Constitution (One Hundred and Third Amendment) Bill.

She thanked the members for their cooperation in the smooth conduction of the House and also expressed her regret if her words or rulings had hurt their sentiments.

The speech was indeed memorable for the subtle suggestions made: "In the last session of the 16th Lok Sabha, it is time that we introspect whether we have lived up to the expectations of the people during the last five years. What we have achieved and what still needs to be done – we should do an impartial analysis," she said while wishing good luck to the members for the ensuing General Elections.

Prime Minister Narendra Modi expressed his respect for Taai in his speech at Indore, "There is only one person who can scold me, and she is Taai!"

□

Lok Sabha speaker Sumitra Mahajan's valedictory speech	
https://www.youtube.com/watch?v=UjxWwz63J9U	

5

With the Times

ताळवेल तानमाने।
प्रबंध कविता जाड वचने।
मज्यासाठी नानाचिह्ने।
सुचती जया॥

Talavela tanamane.
Prabandha kavita jaada vachane.
Majyasathi nanachhinhe.
Suchati jaya.

(Dasbodh, 11.6.8)

(He shows foresight, understands the importance of timing, knows how to compose essays and poetry, and when to use important statements from various texts in appropriate situations. He knows how to use tact in meetings).

—Samarth Ramdas

Sumitra Mahajan was a Speaker with charm and grace. She is sedate, sober and sophisticated; fair, intelligent and cultured; and discerning with her own individualistic style of doing something. Anybody could be impressed by her on first sight and her gentle speech and *sattvic* (pure) demeanour made her the most respected leader in society.

Taai is a connoisseur of all good things in life. Her saris, their texture, design and sweaters worn during winters matched each other. Even though she wore only one sari during the day, she remained neat till evening. If women MPs in Parliament or the employees appreciated her sari, she would smile and admire the response.

Once, in a public interview, a female journalist asked her the secret of her beauty in a light-hearted moment. *Taai* smiled and replied, "I don't use any chemical cosmetics, that's the secret." How true the comment was! Her face is a reflection of her pure heart and clear mind. Though her traditional attire is the sari, she wears Punjabi suits while exercising and at home as she finds them more comfortable to wear. Of course, she prefers suits with a *dupatta* in white or light colours! She is always eager to accept new things that are useful. She is curious, well-read and aware of the technological advances. She is quite comfortable with the new technology – E-mails, online meetings, virtual speeches on zoom, etc.

She is always ready to acquire new technology and therefore wanted the Parliament to be equipped with new technology. Accordingly, she implemented some innovative schemes.

Paperless Parliament

The Ministry of Parliamentary Affairs launched an ambitious project to make the entire proceedings of Parliament and 31 State Assemblies completely paperless. The project was launched in December 2018 during *Taai's* tenure as Speaker.

The objective of the whole project is related to the environment. The use of up-to-date technology is important for environmental protection. The project was prepared and developed in accordance with the rules and procedures of the two Houses.

"Parliament and state assemblies have 5,379 members

who together pose nearly 2 lakh questions every year regarding the functioning of the respective governments. Also, Parliament and state assemblies together present more than 500 committee reports and deal with more than 1700 Bills in a year. In addition to this, more than 10,000 papers are tabled and more than 25,000 notices are given each year. This requires massive paper work, including authentication of documents to be admitted in the respective House. The project was started to get all the work done online. This saved tons of paper and plenty of time.

"Members will be able to submit their questions even by using their mobile phones and the reply will also be made available to them on their phones. And it will be available to other members and general public as well (under RTI Right to Information) at the same time it is presented in the respective Houses.

"As a first step, e-portals have been launched to make both the Houses of Parliament and the Parliament Secretariat paperless. Everything, like submission of notice by a member for asking a question, its acceptance, relevant correspondence with the concerned ministry, and receipt and processing of the information have been made completely online, that is, paperless."

The e-portal make it possible for MPs to access information on Bills, committee meeting schedules, agendas and reports, word-of-mouth debates and other parliamentary suggestions through the e-portal as well as to access 'member reference services' and electronic reference materials.

The 2019 office of the Speaker said in a report: "The e-portal has reduced the number of copies of reports on the House table by 60 per cent. Copies of reports in English version have been reduced by 80 per cent and Hindi versions by 50 per cent. A large amount of paper has been saved and these measures have saved about 2,500 trees. Not only time, energy and money are saved but also protection of environment is ensured.

"As a result of continuous efforts, about 300 lakh papers of A-4 size have been saved, i.e. 80,000 paper rim packets. It saves about two crore rupees every year."

Taai loves to plant trees. She shares a unique bond with them. Every year, on her birthday which falls on April 12, she is seen planting a tree of rare Indian species, such as Kadamba, Rudraksha, Sophiya, Maulshree, Dhak/Palas, etc. in her courtyard and duly takes care of them. Taai likes to walk around the backyard. She stands in front of a tree for a while, talks to it and caresses it. "Trees can feel your emotions. They respond to your love and care," she says.

E-parl

Along with the paperless project, the Parliament Library was digitised and a new portal called E-parl was started for the convenience of the members. As a result, almost all the parliamentary balance sheets are now available at the click of a button. Transparency of Parliament has increased and this is a very necessary and useful step to strengthen a democracy. The responsibility of the people's representatives has increased and it has become clear how active they have been. The details of various development works undertaken by the people's representatives in their respective Lok Sabha constituencies and the questions presented in the Parliament have now become easily available to all. Along with transparency, it naturally has helped to increase their credibility.

It was an ambitious project and had it failed, not only would the hard work been wasted but also the credibility been eroded and the whole process of development would have been reversed. That's what worried *Taai*. That is why she paid special attention to every minute aspect of the project. The stupendous task required an extensive system. It also called for training of MPs, MLAs, their personal assistants, government officials and the staff using the technology. Although the task of supervision was assigned to an independent company, *Taai* regularly ensured that there was coordination between planning and implementation of the project. She also attended to the problems and complaints received from time to time.

Bureau of Parliamentary Studies and Training (BPST)

Media as the watchdog plays a very important role in every democracy. After all, it is the fourth pillar of democracy. It is the means of general communication, information, or entertainment in society. Earlier, only the audio medium – the radio and to some extent newspapers and print medium were the sole means of communication. Later, the audio-visual medium – Doordarshan became important. Over the last twenty to twenty-five years, private channels, including the government media, have become major sources of information.

In her interviews after becoming the Speaker of the Lok Sabha, *Taai* made a general statement that the 'media should act responsibly', though she conscientiously keeps clear of levity or frivolity.

But in the last few years, internal competition and discontentment have increased. In order to increase TRP (Target Rating Point) and satisfy paid news environment in recent years, the trust in the media has taken a drastic hit and because of this, the biggest victim has turned out to be the Indian democracy. This outreach of crony-capitalism in the media is destroying the profession and ethics of journalism. In the last few years, the internal rift and competition in the media has increased so much that *Taai* was forced to lament that in the pursuit of increasing TRP (Target Rating Points), journalists and their employers seem to be turning a blind eye to social commitment and national interests. However, *Taai* relies more on action than on mere words. Therefore, she mainly focuses on the issue of enlightenment of journalists. After she became an MP, *Taai* has been inviting journalists to meals at her home so as to strike a direct and proper dialogue with them. She had also set up a special Indore Haat on the lawns and treated them with special dishes from Indore, such as *dalbafla* and other dishes. It was definitely not persuasion or appeasement, but a sincere desire to establish cordial relations with them.

The Parliamentary Research and Training Institute for Democracies (PRIDE), (earlier called BPST), fell under her jurisdiction.

This institute was set up on 1 January, 1976 as an integral part of the Lok Sabha Secretariat to provide parliamentarians, parliamentary staff and others institutionalised opportunities for systematic training in various disciplines of parliamentary institutions, processes and procedures. The PRIDE`s activities include conducting/organising:

Orientation programmes, lectures and seminars for Members of Parliament and of state legislatures.

Lecture series for Members of Parliament.

Round-table discussions on topical parliamentary themes.

Prof. Hiren Mukerjee Memorial annual parliamentary lecture.

Training, Attachment and study visits/tours of presiding officers, members and officers of foreign Parliaments.· International training programmes, held annually, for foreign parliamentary officials, viz. Parliamentary Internship Programme and International

Training Programme in legislative drafting.

Orientation programmes and seminars for media personnel accredited to the Press galleries of Parliament.

Appreciation courses for probationers of All India and Central Services and middle-level officers of the Government of India.

Study visits for government officers, academics, scholars, students and others.

Training, attachment and study tour opportunities for parliamentary officials from India to foreign Parliaments and training institutions.

Taai observed that the local reporters in Indore asked less questions about the country as they hardly had any experience of the country's political situation. She undertook many initiatives through BPST to enable district-level journalists to get a glimpse of the political environment and experience of Delhi.

The Lok Sabha Secretariat, under the auspices of BPST, arranged for a number of publications for journalists, including the publication of information leaflets and literature aimed at providing information related to the proceedings of the Lok Sabha. A number of awareness programmes were organised which benefited 435 journalists and media persons from 23 states.

These awareness programmes have made it easier for media persons to inform the general public about the proceedings of the Lok Sabha and the Vidhan Sabha. Liaising with Parliament and the legislature provided an opportunity to transmit information and act as a true medium. The press also succeeded in taking their work to the people.

In addition, special training programmes were organised for the officers/staff and people's representatives working in Parliaments/legislatures of different countries. Secretariat staff/officers were sent abroad for similar training so that they could learn some of the best traditions of the Parliaments of other countries.

During her tenure, *Taai* cherished some good cultural and social traditions. The list is interesting and distinctive:

- Do not visit anybody empty-handed.
- Do not send the visitor empty-handed. Generally, she gifted books to visitors. Some of her favourite books included *Suraj Samhita, Ek hota Carver*, etc.
- *Taai* enjoyed the festive atmosphere and celebrated Gudi Padwa enthusiastically in the Parliament House. On that day, everyone enjoyed a treat of *shrikhand-puri* in the afternoon. She took pleasure in all the celebrations and had informal chats with the guests.
- *Taai's* love for literature, art and drama is well known. Many organisations held their cultural programmes in Delhi. *Taai* made it a point to attend the programmes whenever possible and praise the artistes and organisers. This would encourage them and boost their confidence and enthusiasm. *Taai* used her love for good literature in Parliament and organised many interesting plays and cultural programmes during the time of the convention and the plays included Manoj Joshi's *Chanakya, Chakravyuha* by Nitish Bharadwaj, Pushkar Shrotri's award-winning film *Tumbatu,* based on a true story of Uganda. She used them as a means to achieve the broader goal of familiarising the MPs with the best works of art in the country. Art and culture flourish if scholars and artists are given due recognition. They get a glimpse of reality, understand new ideas and concepts and get inspired to implement them in society. It helps to make the society more civilised.
- *Taai* would call many people at home for tea;

sometimes she would also call the families also and have informal chats with them. Going beyond politics, she would initiate dialogues with the families. This helped her to develop personal relations with many MPs. She would exchange pleasantries to develop intimacy with the family. One such enjoyable incident was when she invited Mrs. Sonia Gandhi and Priyanka Gandhi for tea. *Taai* simply enjoyed all the false pouting and sulking between the mother and daughter and this included a funny incident when a daughter tried to make cake for the mother! Later Priyanka Gandhi often sent different recipes prepared by her to *Taai*. She had even baked a lovely cake for *Taai's* granddaughter.

- *Taai* was a good communicator. A popular leader of the Opposition party once wondered, "*Taai*, I could not persuade my daughter-in-law, but how could you convince her in just 10 minutes?"

It so happened that his daughter-in-law was also an MP and a famous sportsperson. She was bold, carefree and did not pay much attention to her dressing style. During one such informal chat, *Taai* very diplomatically advised her, "We are in politics, thousands of people watch us. Many women consider us as their role models. Hence we should be cautious about our behaviour and careful about our clothes in public life. It really helps us professionally." The daughter-in-law was so convinced by *Taai's* advice that she promptly introduced the necessary changes in her dressing style and behaviour.

- 'Dialogue with MP' was another successful programme under which informal meetings were held with young and newly appointed MPs. *Taai* not only got to know the hopes and aspirations of new MPs but also could explain in detail about who made maximum use provisions of the question-hour session, zero hour, private Member Bill, etc. and also clarified some inner complications.

- *Taai* also invited some newly married MPs along with their spouses for dinner. Some of her guests included Shrikant Shinde, Deependra Singh Hooda, Dushyant Chautala, Conrad Kongkal Sangma (son of erstwhile Chief Minister of Mehgalaya, P.A. Sangma) and also offered some useful tips. She gifted them a copy each of the Constitution. Deependra Singh Hooda was simply thrilled to see the signatures of his grandfather Ranbir Singh Hooda, who was a member of the committee constituted for drafting the Constitution. He profusely thanked *Taai* for the precious gift. Thence onwards his relations with *Taai* developed so deep that he always shared family problems with her.
- April 12 is *Taai's* birthday and everybody knew that *Taai* did not like grand celebrations and celebrated by planting saplings. She made an exception once when the Lok Sabha session was on. As soon as *Taai* entered the Lok Sabha, she was surprised to see the House transformed into a school classroom. Everyone began to sing, "Happy birthday to you." *Taai* laughed in embarrassment and silenced everyone by taking a sweet revenge by offering sweets!
- *Taai* cared a lot for 'differently abled' people. The Yuvak Pratishthan had provided assistance for the rehabilitation of injured and disabled persons during the terrorist attacks. The president of the Youth Foundation, Kirit Somaiya told *Taai* about their wish to see the Parliament. She immediately organised a discussion with them in the Parliament House. Prime Minister Narendra Modi also joined them. *Taai* spoke kindly to all of them and invited them for lunch. She

was a perfect host to them.

- *Taai* is disciplined and maintenance of protocol has been her priority. Once she arrived late for the function due to some health issues. She was expected to arrive before the President but reached late at the venue. She felt very embarrassed and apologised to the audience. The next day she took an official appointment from the President's office and went and apologised to the President. She believed in maintaining the honour and dignity of the post.
- *Taai* gave active support to the South Asian Speakers' Summit. The concept of the annual summit was mooted during the first South Asian Speakers; Summit held in 2016 at Dhaka, Bangladesh. *Taai* had promoted and shaped the idea of an annual summit. Earlier such events were organised in the national capital, but *Taai* chose to hold such conferences in other major cities of the country too. Thus, the second summit was held at Indore in 2017, while the third summit was held in 2018 at Colombo, Sri Lanka. The next conference was scheduled to be held in Pakistan, but when Pakistan did not invite Bangladesh, *Taai* did not like it and notified it. Later, Pakistan adopted a policy of deferment and the summit was cancelled.
- Kavinder Gupta, the Speaker of the Jammu & Kashmir Assembly, was not invited by Pakistan for the Commonwealth Parliamentary Union meeting at Islamabad, so (File photo) India threatened to boycott the event.

Lok Sabha Speaker Sumitra Mahajan called a meeting of the Speakers and Chairmen of all state assemblies where it was unanimously decided to boycott the event. She had said that the Chairman of the CPA would be requested to use his good offices to immediately resolve the matter arising out of the unilateral decision of Pakistan, failing which India and its assemblies will boycott the event.

The headquarters of the Commonwealth Parliamentary Association (CPA) announced that the Commonwealth Parliamentary Conference to be held in Islamabad had been cancelled by the CPA after a tough stance taken by India against Pakistan's decision not to invite the Speaker of the Jammu & Kashmir legislature to the meet.

The unilateral decision of Pakistan violated the provisions of the CPA Constitution and this was recognised by the UK-based CPA Secretariat and the Chairperson of its Executive Committee.

"It is wrong (on the part of Pakistan). They cited an old rule of 1951-57 regarding their having raised an issue in the UN Security Council for not inviting J&K Speaker," she said, adding it had lost its relevance now.

The Speaker said Pakistan gave this reply when India took up the matter strongly with the CPA Chairperson and Secretary General against leaving out the J&K Speaker.

Mahajan made it clear that to ensure participation of the Speaker of Lok Sabha and those of other state assemblies, J&K Speaker will have to be invited or the venue should be changed to some other country.

The resolution said Pakistani decision violate the "provisions of the CPA Constitution, keeping the Executive Committee and the General Assembly of CPA in the dark while acting against the century-old tradition of CPA which is a membership organisation that has constitutionally been bound to invite all its member branches to the CPA annual conference so long as a branch is in good financial standing with the association."

The meet resolved to call upon Dr. Shirin Chaudhury, Speaker of Bangladesh Parliament and Chairperson of the CPA Executive Committee to use her good offices to immediately resolve the matter and ensure issue of invitation to the Jammu &Kashmir 'CPA Branch' failing which 'CPA India Region' including the Union and State Branches (will) boycott the 61st Commonwealth Parliamentary Conference in Islamabad, Pakistan.

Later the CPA Executive Committee, cancelled the 61st Commonwealth Parliamentary Conference (CPC) slated for Islamabad, Pakistan. This followed an emergency teleconference meeting of the Executive Committee convened to consider the Pakistan Branch's refusal to invite the Jammu & Kashmir Branch to the conference.

No Commonwealth Parliamentary Conference was held in 2015 but the 61st General Assembly was convened by the CPA Executive Committee.

The tough stand taken by India increased India's prestige in international circles.

Taai had to face many such moments of pride, happiness and also some depressing ones.

□

6

Distressed...Gloomy...Pensive...

संगीत (बरोबर) चालिता तरी व्याप।
नाही तर अवघाचि संताप।
क्षण क्षणा विक्षेप किती।
म्हणोनि सांगावे॥

Sangeeta (barobar) chalita tari vyapa.
Nahi tara avaghachi santapa.
Kshana kshana vikshepa kiti.
Mhanoni sangave.

(Dasbodh, 19.7.25)

(To ensure smooth running of everything calls for hard work, and if things do not turn out well, it creates a lot of dissent and anger among people at every moment. There are many obstacles to success, but how many of them can be enumerated?)

—Samarth Ramdas

While handling the position of the Speaker of Lok Sabha, Sumitrataai had her share of trying times over the years. There were many ups and downs. Success came her way quite often, yet sometimes unhappiness did engulf her. *Taai*, who has been active in socio- political activities since 1980, and electoral politics after that and was nominated as elderman in

Indore Municipal corporation in 1984; has mastered the art of 'switch on and switch off' in life. She has learnt to cope with stress and look forward in life. However, some annoying pangs of disappointments and pain did find their place.

The death of E. Ahamed was one such incident. Here is the account based on the report of the proceedings by the office of the Speaker of Lok Sabha:

Date: January 30, 2017, 11 a.m.

Place: Sansad Bhavan

Subject: Preparation session on the Budget to be presented in Lok Sabha on February 1, 2017

Taai presided over the meeting. Shri E. Ahamed, a senior Member of Parliament from Kerala and the president of the Indian Union Muslim League reached the meeting a little late. He was not looking fully fit. *Taai* asked him about his well-being and advised, "You should have taken some rest today. Do not exert yourself. You are not looking fresh." He smiled slightly and evaded the topic.

Date: January 31, 2017, 11 a.m.

Place: Central Hall of Parliament

Subject: Pre-budget economic survey session

Hon'ble President Shri Pranab Mukherjee's address to the joint sessions of both Houses of Parliament. The pre-Budget economic survey would be tabled.

The session began with the Hon'ble President's address to the joint session of both Houses of Parliament. Shri E. Ahamed reached when the President was delivering the address. The Central Hall was full. Thus, Shri Ahamed occupied the seat at the back where some additional chairs were arranged. As per rules, *Taai* was sitting on the dais to the left of the Hon'ble President. She could have the entire view of the Central Hall. As *Taai* is always alert, she could sense some problem at the back. She realised that some member was not feeling well. The speech was delivered. The day's proceedings were concluded. *Taai* came to know that Shri E. Ahamed collapsed in Parliament and was rushed to Ram Manohar Lohia (RML) Hospital. He was admitted in the Intensive Care Unit (ICU).

Taai came to her chamber and grasped all the information about the incident. She was quite worried about the health of Shri E. Ahamed. It was quite natural, indeed!

Shri Edappakath Ahamed alias E. Ahamed was her contemporary, of the same age, equivalent and her associate in Lok Sabha since 1991. He represented the Malappuram Lok Sabha constituency of Kerala and was the National President of the Indian Union Muslim League (IUML) from 2008 till his death in 2017.

After India became independent, All India Muslim League was formally disbanded and the Indian Union Muslim League (IUML) came into existence from March 10, 1948. It was legally established on September 1, 1951. Since then, it always had a constant, albeit small, presence in the Lok Sabha. Along with Kerala, it has its representatives in the state government of West Bengal. Likewise, it has its followers in the states of Tamil Nadu, Puducherry, Maharashtra, Karnataka, Uttar Pradesh and Assam. It has its representation to some extent in Sthanik Swarajya Sanstha also.

Shri E. Ahamed was an active member of the IUML right from its establishment. He was elected to the Kerala Legislative Assembly for five times from 1967 to 1987.

He was elected to the Lok Sabha from 1991 to 2009 and served as Minister of State for External Affairs in the Manmohan Singh government. Shri Ahamed represented India in the United Nations 10 times. He was included as the representative of India in the United Nations even in Vajpayee-led government.

A lawyer by profession, Shri E. Ahamed was a serious-minded and studious politician. He has four books to his credit. Thus, it was but natural for *Taai* to be anxious about her long-time associate.

As the Speaker of Lok Sabha, she was also worried about facing a constitutional problem. She visited Ram Manohar

Hospital and inquired about Shri E. Ahamed's health. He was critical and was on ventilator. His son and daughter had departed from Kerala. The further decision was to be taken once they reached the hospital.

Taai sensed the grim reality. She was bothered by a hypothetical question: Can the government continue presenting the Budget if a sitting Lok Sabha MP dies? The process was set in motion soon.

She immediately contacted Parliament Affairs Minister Shri Ananth Kumar and other constitution experts and had a detailed discussion with them. She called her associates and explained the gravity of the situation. Shri E. Ahamed was a sitting MP. If a sitting MP dies while the Parliament session is on, then by convention the House had to be adjourned for a day. The main reason is definitely to express respect towards the departed MP and also because many associates and colleagues have to attend the funeral. If her fear became a reality, then Lok Sabha had to be adjourned but the Hon'ble President had already signed the pre-Budget economic survey. The date was printed on it. There was also apprehension that the Budget may get leaked if delayed, as it had been printed for distribution. The secrecy of Budget was also important. The collection of taxes would be affected and cause a great loss. Share market depended on it and could lead to fluctuations in transactions. At the same time, it would be against humanity not to adjourn the Lok Sabha. *Taai* was in a dilemma. She asked the assistant officers to investigate if such an incident had occurred earlier and what was the action taken by the government?

Many journalists and representatives of news channels were waiting outside the hospital. Live telecast on the various channels continued with arguments and counter arguments on the issue.

Taai was awake all night. She was restless, tense and worried. She was under tremendous pressure as the government was keen on presenting the Budget while the media and Opposition were insisting on adjourning the House. Around 12.30 a.m., the officers could find the Parliament data of 1955-56, when a similar incident had occurred. The Congress party was in power. A sitting Congress MP died on the day of Budget and the House proceedings were held as scheduled.

February 1, 2017, 7.30 a.m.

Taai's residence, 20 Akbar Road

The officers informed *Taai* about the past precedent in the morning. *Taai* was annoyed that why she was not informed at night; however, she was also relieved. Armed with the legal inputs from the experts and past precedents, she had made up her mind.

February 1, 2017, 9 a.m.

Taai's residence

Office, 20 Akbar Road

The news came that 78-year-old sitting MP Shri E. Ahamed passed away at 2.15 a.m. The family members immediately declared that the dead body would be taken to his home town in Kerala for burial.

The journalists and representatives of various channels were busy telecasting arguments and counter-arguments as per their needs.

February 1, 2017, 10 a.m.

Taai went to Shri E. Ahamed's residence to pay homage to the departed soul. From there she went to Parliament House. In the meantime, she contacted all the party members. "We will face the situation together. It is binding by constitution to present the Budget in the house. It is not possible to adjourn the house. Please cooperate; I will manage everything," she assured. Some MPs from Kerala were disappointed, but all were aware of the helplessness of the situation. Thus, it was felt that the things could be coped with.

February 1, 2017, 11 a.m.

Sansad Bhavan, Lok Sabha

Paying homage to Shri E Ahamed, Finance Minister Arun Jaitley presented the Union Budget.

Speaker Sumitra Mahajan said, "Hon'ble members, as you are aware that in the event of death of a sitting Member, the House is adjourned for the day as a mark of respect after the obituary reference to the passing away of the Member is made in the House. I would have adjourned the House for the day, but today's sitting has been specifically fixed by the Hon'ble President for presentation of the Union Budget for the financial year 2017-18, which is a constitutional obligation. In view of this exceptional situation, the House may go ahead with the presentation of the Union Budget for 2017-18. However, the House would not sit tomorrow as a mark of respect to the departed soul."

> *Parliament data showed that on July 31, 1974, Lok Sabha speaker Gurdial Singh Dhillon did not adjourn the House after the death of a minister, M.B. Rana. He allowed the then Finance Minister Y.B. Chavan to present the Budget. On April 19, 1954, sitting MP, J.P. Soren, died on the day of the Railway Budget but the House proceedings were held as scheduled. On both the occasions, the House was adjourned as a mark of respect and reconvened within hours, for the Budget.*

February 2, 2017: As declared earlier, the House was adjourned.

No proceedings took place.

February 3, 2017, 11 a.m.

Sansad Bhawan, Lok Sabha

Zero-hour question-answer session. Congress leader Shri Mallikarjun Kharge raised the issue of not adjourning Lok Sabha on the death of Shri E. Ahamed. He alleged there was a delay in removing the ventilator and in declaring his death. BJP members started talking passionately.

On Monday not much work was done during the question-answer session in Lok Sabha because, the Opposition members repeatedly demanded a probe into the manner in which the death of Ahamed was 'handled' by the government. Congress and left MPs rushed to the 'well'. Even after the general proceedings resumed in the afternoon when discussion was initiated on motion of thanks for President's address, Congress president, Shrimati Sonia Gandhi staged a walk-out. After staging a symbolical protest, the Opposition leaders returned to the House after some time.

The Opposition leaders staged protests near the statue of Mahatma Gandhi in Parliament premises. Many leaders participated in it. There were arguments and counter arguments. MPs from Kerala noted their protests. Shri E. Ahamed was a veteran political leader from Kerala and president of Muslim League. The media was targeting *Taai*.

There were repeated allegations as Shri E. Ahamed was an Opposition leader and a Muslim.

Congress vice president, Rahul Gandhi, joined the protest at Parliament complex over the controversy surrounding IUML MP, E. Ahamed's death.

Taai was quite hurt on the day. She does not have a habit of writing a diary every day, but occasionally she does pen down her thoughts. Thus, dismayed by the turn of events that day, she expressed her thoughts in a diary.

"Electoral politics overrode the expected maturity by years of experience of governance?

It was decided on February 1, what was the need to raise the issue again on February 3? Was it right to criticise the government? But who thinks about what is appropriate and what is improper? They seem to be more interested in trampling upon somebody... political unsettling... arguments... counter arguments... demeaning the opponents? Is it right to make use of Lok Sabha like this? ... We tend to forget just that. ....the way we are using somebody's death for some selfish interests...oh, no, everything is so perturbing, depressing – the same thought again and again. Am I lacking somewhere? What is my role? As a Speaker, if it is my duty to convince members of different parties regarding smooth operations and making them aware of their responsibilities, then I am definitely lacking somewhere.

The whole procedure of politics is so tainted, so ruined!

I, who always took precautions not to utter any personal criticism against a contestant even during elections – believed to ask votes on the basis of work – who always strived not to resort to wrong means to achieve anything – who remained in politics with a firm belief in explaining, convincing everybody... Perhaps I am becoming inept, useless, outdated now....

Anyways...Today I am dejected – restless. It feels very melancholic and unsettled."

□

Distressed.. gloomy..pensive..	
me-qr.com	

7

Of 'Hug and Wink'

राखो जाणे नितीन्याय।
न करी न करवी अन्याये।
कठीण प्रसंगी उपायें।
करू जाणे॥

Rakho jane nitinyaye.
Na kari na karavi anyaye.
Kathina prasangi upaye.
Karu jane.

(Dasbodh 11.6.18)

(He knows how to grant justice and adopt morality. Neither does he do any injustice to anyone nor does he allow others to do it. He knows how to solve difficult problems).

—Samarth Ramdas

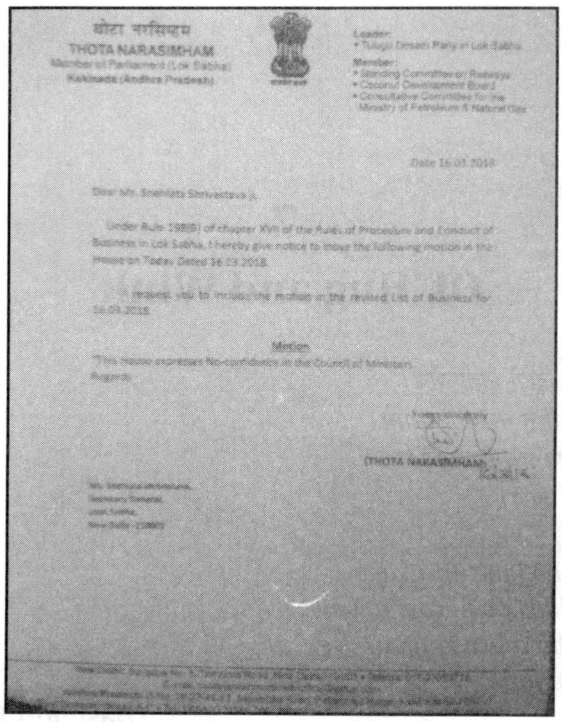

THOTA NARASIMHAM
Member of Parliament (Lok Sabha)
Kakinada (Andhra Pradesh)

Leader:
• Telugu Desam Party in Lok Sabha
Member:
• Standing Committee on Railways
• Coconut Development Board
• Consultative Committee for the Ministry of Petroleum & Natural Gas

Date 16.03.2018

Dear Ms. Snehlata Shrivastava ji,

Under Rule 198(B) of chapter XVII of the Rules of Procedure and Conduct of Business in Lok Sabha, I hereby give notice to move the following motion in the House on Today Dated 16.03.2018.

I request you to include the motion in the revised List of Business for 16.03.2018.

Motion

"This House expresses No-confidence in the Council of Ministers.

Regards

Yours sincerely

(THOTA NARASIMHAM)

Image of a No Confidence motion notice

Date: 16 March, 2018

Dear Ms Snehlata Shrivastavaji,

Under Rule 198 (b) of Chapter XVII of the Rules of Procedure and Conduct of Business in Lok Sabha. I hereby give notice to move the following motion in the House today dated 6-03-2018.

Motion

The House expresses no-confidence in the Council of Ministers

s/d

(Thota Narasimham)

The Telugu Desam Party (TDP) MP, Thota Narasimham submitted a letter to the then Lok Sabha Secretary General, Shrimati Snehlata Shrivastava, seeking permission to move a no-confidence motion against the Narendra Modi government. All Opposition parties decided to support it.

It was felt that the no-confidence motion against the government would come for discussion in the beginning of the forthcoming 2018 monsoon session. The Lok Sabha Speaker Shrimati Sumitra Mahajan admitted the motion. Parliamentary Affairs Minister Shri Ananth Kumar informed immediately that the government is ready to face the no-confidence motion.

On July 18, 2018 during the question-answer session, TDP's Kesineri Shrinivas raised the issue that it has moved a no-confidence motion against the Narendra Modi government for not giving special package to Andhra Pradesh. He moved the motion before all the MPs and then it came forward for discussion.

The constitution gives right to the Opposition parties to move the no-confidence motion against the government. It was 27th no-confidence motion in the history of Indian constitution. Before this, in 2003, the Congress, with the help of other Opposition parties, had brought a motion of no-confidence against the Atal Bihari Vajpayee-led NDA. The NDA government comfortably defeated the Opposition in the no-confidence motion. The no-confidence motion in the year 1999 brought down the National Democratic Alliance (NDA) government led by Atal Bihari Vajpayee by just one vote. Thus, in 2018, it was interesting to see the outcome of the no-confidence motion.

Actually N. Chandrababu Naidu of TDP was a strong supporter of NDA government but Naidu was disenchanted with the BJP government over refusal to grant special-category status to Andhra. The TDP's growing rift with the

NDA reached a critical point. It withdrew its support to NDA government and moved the no-confidence motion.

Normally, during the discussion, all the work done by the government or not done is reviewed. A survey comes before the public. The ordinary citizens take it very seriously. In a way it is a test of the government. There is a whip (a *fatwa*) that requires all members to be present; that is why the House is full. The rules are strict. Leaders of the Opposition are in an aggressive mood to attack the ruling party. Every party is allotted a stipulated time. It is essential to give to the Speaker the names of the leaders who would speak. The exact strategy of who, what and how to speak is chalked out. Every word is carefully spoken.

On July 20, Rahul Gandhi was to speak on behalf of the Congress party.

Rahul Gandhi is not a seasoned politician, nor a scholarly MP and not an efficient orator either. Till then, out of 125 lakh questions asked in the question-answer hour, not a single question was asked by Rahul Gandhi. His presence in the Lok Sabha was only 52 per cent. Moreover, if a member is to remain absent, then he has to take permission from the Speaker. During the initial period of the Lok Sabha, Rahul Gandhi suddenly went abroad for one-and-a-half months. Ethics Committee may have to consider to investigate it. But *Taai* was quite considerate then. Firstly, she sent a message to Shrimati Sonia Gandhi through Shri Mallikarjun Khargeji, to send a note regarding Rahul Gandhi's absence. Since there was no action, she sent a message through Shri Jyotiraditya Scindia, who was Rahul Gandhi's friend then. Immediately Soniaji gave the required letter and the subject was closed there.

Rahul Gandhi participated in the debate on no-confidence motion. He spoke for 32 minutes out of 38 minutes allotted to the Congress party. All the MPs in the House were restless.

There were attacks and counter attacks. Prime Minister Narendra Modi was quietly listening to the speech. The unique characteristic of the Prime Minister is that he patiently listens to everything that is said without uttering a word, without looking at any papers. Rahul Gandhi ended his speech. Lok Sabha Speaker Sumitra Mahajan was about to call the name of the next speaker, when all of a sudden, Rahul Gandhi walked across the aisle, walked up to Prime Minister Narendra Modi and hugged him.

Everyone was stunned. *Taai* composed herself and said, "This is not necessary....no...it is not required..." The Prime Minister was taken aback at first and gestured as if asking Gandhi why he was there. After recovering from an apparent shock moment, the Prime Minister called Gandhi back towards him and the two shook hands. He patted Rahul Gandhi on his back and exchanged a word or two with him, smilingly. Then Rahul Gandhi returned to his seat, continued with his speech and later winked and smiled.

Those inside the Lok Sabha were shocked and surprised. What they had seen had not happened inside Parliament ever before.

So were the people who saw what happened on their TV screens. And the media of course got a ready and sensational opportunity!

Taai says, "I didn't know what was happening. What do I say to this? How should I control the House? Really, I was unable to understand. I was looking at Modiji. I hoped he would not get up from his seat. I was relieved when he did not move from his seat. I thought not to drag the issue further and continued the session. Later I declared the lunch-break."

But Sumitra Mahajan's challenges weren't over with this.

The proceedings began after the lunch-break. The voting was at 6 p.m. Everyone was busy and hoping that everything would go on smoothly. Then Home Minister Rajnath Singh stood to speak and referred to the hug act, "*Sadan me chipko andolan chalu kiya hai*" (a Chipko movement has been initiated in the House). The entire Opposition turned furious. Congress leader Mallikarjun Kharge started speaking animatedly. The issue should have been ignored, but Rajnath Singh commented on it. This did not amuse Lok Sabha Speaker Sumitra Mahajan. She immediately intervened. Every member did not want to lose the opportunity and wanted to speak. They demanded extra time; blamed the government for injustice and being biased. There was total confusion and chaos.

The situation was getting out of control. *Taai* was very angry. She reprimanded, "This is not proper. This should not happen in the House. We should act in a civilised manner here. The House has its own set of rules that has to be followed. There should not be a breach of propriety. The decorum of the House should be maintained at all cost."

However, Kharge was repeatedly speaking. *Taai* scolded him, "You were not present in the House; you have not witnessed the incident. If you were here, even you would not have liked it. He is the Prime Minister. There is a decorum (that we attach) to the Prime Minister's post. The Prime Minister was sitting in the House in his capacity as the PM and not as Narendra Modi. Every member must maintain decorum and dignity of the House because no one else will. I want everybody to co-exist peacefully.

"People have elected us as their representatives. They have given us this honour. We should respect their opinion. It is not just my responsibility, but it is the duty of every single member of the House," she said, referring to all the members in the House.

Still the uproar continued.

Taai was a little annoyed, "I have no enmity with Rahulji. Even I feel he has to achieve many things in his political career. Let his leadership grow further and further. He is like my son and it is my duty as a mother to correct him, teach him what is proper and what is not."

However, the MPs refused to be quiet.

Then *Taai* schooled the parliamentarians, "Why will I oppose hugging? It is good to have cordial relations with everybody. It helps to do the work easily. But there is certain decorum - certain rules - about how and where to do the act. No one should act against the decorum of the House. You admire Modiji, I accept it. I understand the emotions. You can go to his house, meet him, chat with him. You can express your emotions there; but not at this place. Here the Prime Minister was sitting in the House in his capacity as the PM, the supreme leader of the country. We should keep this in mind before making any move or gesture.

"The way it happened was beyond any reason. Actually, the hugging was not proper; when Rahulji returned to his seat, started speaking again and winked. But this was a step too much. This will not be permitted in the House. I will not allow it. I request you again and again that the House will work as per the rules. I request all of you to sit quietly."

Taai maintained her calm and gained control over the House and resumed the proceedings.

Instead of the usual soft and sober Sumitrataai, the House witnessed a different image of *Taai*– firm, strong, strict and tough.

□

8
Determined and Vigilant

मुख्य हरिकथा निरुपण।
दुसरे ते राजकारण।
तिसरे अत्यंत सावधपण।
सर्वांविषयी॥

चौथा अत्यंत साक्षेप।
फेडावे नाना आक्षेप।
अन्याये थोर अथवा।
अल्प क्षमा करीत जावे॥

Mukhya Harikathaa Nirupana.
Dusare te rajakarana.
Tisare atyanta savadhapana.
SarvanvishayiII

Chautha atyanta sakshepa.
Phedave nana akshepa.
Anyaye thora athava.
Alpa kshama karita jave.

(Dasbodh, 11.5.5)

(Most important are the explanations and narrations about God. After that, importance should be given to politics.

Thirdly, one should be attentive in all matters.

Fourthly, every effort should be made to satisfy all arguments and misconceptions that others may have, and the injustices or offences committed by someone, be they small or large, ought to be forgiven).

—Samarth Ramdas

Rulers should always be alert. Any kind of relaxation, delay or neglect of an issue may cause endless troubles to the common people. And as time passes, the situation worsens, the problem turns acute and then it becomes too difficult to solve.

Lok Sabha Speaker, Sumitra Mahajan, had to face an international strategic impasse during her tenure. Soon after becoming the Prime Minister of the country, Narendra Modi not only concentrated on the internal affairs of the country but also laid emphasis on maintaining good relations between India and the neighbouring countries.

There was a 40-year-old dispute related to India's closest neighbor, Bangladesh, over fixing the international boundaries between the two countries. It was a geographical as well as emotional issue, serious and complicated.

The subject came before Taai in 2014.

As per Taai's nature, she started studying the matter in detail and also tried to understand the nuances of the issue clearly.

India is bordered by Sri Lanka, Pakistan, Afghanistan, Nepal, China, Myanmar and Bangladesh. All share boundaries. This means that these countries are India's neighbours. Some are simply connected by land; some are connected only by sea, while others are connected by both land and sea. The longest border line with Bangladesh is 4096.70 kms long (2,545 miles). It is the land boundary with forests in it. The triangle of the Ganges has the Sunderbans, where the land and its edges constantly keep changing. This area is made up of many islands due to being the delta of River Ganges. Entire Bangladesh is surrounded by the Indian states of West Bengal, Assam, Meghalaya, Tripura and Mizoram. Only a small part of it lies adjacent to Myanmar. There is no such thing as an international border because it is basically an unnatural division.

Many of these villages are such that it is not exactly clear in which country they are. Moreover, the villages are not unified but are divided; in some cases, the houses are in India, while lands, shops, etc. are in Bangladesh or vice versa.

In some cases, the village is in one country and the police station is in another country.

As many as 162 areas are small towns, villages, which are called chittmahal in the local language; these settlements and its 51,549 residents have been waiting for their basic human rights since 1974.

Taai was shocked and disturbed by the carelessness of the governments of both the countries. "How can they play with the lives of the people? No strategy, no foresight! Simply because they do not mingle in society, do not identify themselves with masses. Those who want to work for society or country, should be completely integrated with the masses, like Prabhu Ramchandra," she said.

India and Bangladesh had a dispute regarding maritime borders but which has been resolved now. India and Bangladesh had been engaged in long drawn-out and inconclusive negotiations on the delimitation of their maritime boundary since 1974, when eight rounds of talks were held on bilateral negotiations. Finally, in October 2009, Bangladesh issued a notice of arbitration proceedings under the United Nations Convention on the Law of the Sea for the Demarcation of the Maritime Boundary. The Arbitration Tribunal was set up under the Permanent Court of Arbitration (PCA) in The Hague, in the matter of Bay of Bengal Maritime Boundary Delimitation between India and Bangladesh.

As per the ruling of the tribunal delivered on July 7, 2014, four-fifths of the disputed maritime boundary of 25,602 square kms, that is 9,467 square kms of maritime territory was given to Bangladesh. This decision recognised the sovereign rights of Bangladesh over the marine resources of the continental region.

The only satisfactory point for India was that it was given New Moore Island.

The island is located between the Satkhira district of Bangladesh and the South 24 Parganas district of West Bengal, on the international border near the shallow coast, where River Hariabhanga meets the Bay of Bengal. The island, with a circumference of about 2 kms, is also known as the South Talapatti and Purvasha Island. It was a small, secluded, offshore, sandbar-type of island, off the coast of the Bay of Bengal and at the mouth of the Ganga-Brahmaputra delta. It originated suddenly in the Bay of Bengal after Hurricane Bhola lashed the area in November 1970 and disappeared around March 2010. It is now submerged in the Bay of Bengal, but two things were important about this island.

India for the first time hoisted the Indian flag on the island in 1981 and established a temporary base of the Border Security Forces (BSF), regularly visiting with naval gunships. According to the Radcliffe Boundary (a boundary line declared in 1947 between East Pakistan and India), it is known as the maritime part of India within the international border. It is important from the defence point of view.

The arbitral tribunal granted India a division of about 6,000 sq km where the island once existed. One of the creeks that India explored for natural gas in 2006 is located 50kms south of the mouth of the Hariabhanga river, near New Moore Island.

Many petroleum companies were reluctant to explore oil and gas because of the controversy. Some companies even withdrew after making the initial investments. In December 2013, the Australian firm called Santos withdrew from two C-blocs, citing the reasons of security and maritime disputes with Bangladesh.

But now that India has the ownership of the entire region, it became possible for the Indian government to set a long-term goal for economic development of the region in the Bay of Bengal. Against this background, it was necessary to negotiate with Bangladesh and resolve the land demarcation issue amicably. It was not that there had been no previous attempts, but the Indian government had not taken any concrete steps and was satisfied with taking temporary steps. Thus, people from the area were quite distressed and disappointed.

- The Indo-Pak war resulted in the formation of Bangladesh in 1971.
- An agreement was reached between the two countries on May 16, 1974 to demarcate the border between the two countries.
- The issue was discussed time and again.
- Some temporary reforms were introduced in both the countries, e.g. citizens were allowed to travel between both the countries from 9 a.m. to 5 p.m. Movement of vehicles, such as bicycle, rickshaw, bullock cart, etc. was allowed between the two countries. Correspondence regarding this was held between the countries on 6 September, 2011.
- On December 18, 2013, the then Minister of External

Affairs, Salman Khurshid introduced a Bill in the Rajya Sabha and it was referred to the Standing Committee of Parliament on December 31, 2013. But nothing happened afterwards. Elections were held and there was change of power at the Centre.

On the whole, the issue was postponed.

Background

In 1971, under the leadership of Sheikh Mujibur Rehman, Bangladesh came into being as a result of the Indo-Pakistan war and Pakistan got divided. The Bangladeshis were indebted to India for that. However, things have changed a lot since then.

- Assam remained disturbed from 1979 to 2005 due to illegal infiltration of Bangladeshi nationals into Assam.
- The whole of northeast India was engulfed by terrorism. These terroristic activities got support from Bangladesh.
- Attempts were made to separate the entire northeastern part of India, known as the Seven Sisters, from India.

Failure to get Assam included in East Pakistan in 1947 remained a source of abiding resentment in Pakistan and later in Bangladesh also. It was often vocalised openly as well.

Zulfiqar Ali Bhutto, in his book, Myths of Independence has written, "It would be wrong to think that Kashmir is the only dispute that divides India and Pakistan, though undoubtedly the most significant. One at least is as nearly important as the Kashmir dispute is that of Assam and some districts of India adjacent to East Pakistan. To this, Pakistan has very good claims."

Even the more pro-India leaders like Sheikh Mujibur Rehman, in his book, Eastern Pakistan– its Population and Economics has asserted, "East Pakistan must have sufficient land for its expansion and because Assam has abundant forests, mineral resources, coal, petroleum etc., East Pakistan must include Assam to be economically and financially strong."

- Dissatisfaction persisted in Pakistan as Assam could not be annexed to East Pakistan in 1947 and Bangladesh had an eye on northeast India. As a result, terrorist activities erupted. The Naxalite movement gained momentum. Many innocent civilians were killed. Heroic soldiers had to be martyred. Political instability ensued. The pace of development slowed down and the attitude of the people towards the Central Government became tainted. Separatism and provincialism became the subject of identity. Nationalism turned secondary. That is why it was very difficult for the government to deal with the issue.

The ruling party did not have the courage to make timely decisions.

The 2011 Protocol, signed between Manmohan Singh of India and Sheikh Hasina of Bangladesh agreed to maintain the status quo in addressing the issue of adverse possession of land. According to the Protocol, India would receive 2,777,038 acres of land from Bangladesh and in turn, transfer 2,267,682 acres of land to Bangladesh. The 2011 protocol was made an accord with the state governments of Assam, Meghalaya, Tripura and West Bengal but could not be implemented due to adverse political circumstances.

After the change of power at the Centre, the BJP-led

Hon'ble Prime Minister Shri Narendra Modiji releasing the book 'Matoshree', a play penned by Taai on the life of Punyashlok Ahilyadevi Holkar

Exchanging thoughts with late Shri Atal Bihari Vajpayeeji

Offering flowers on the statue of Punyashlok Ahilyabai Holkar installed in Parliament

Pleasing moments of marital bliss—Shri Jayant Mahajan and Sumitra Taai

Jubilant Mahajan family

In a serious discussion with Shri Lal Krishna Advaniji

From 2 to 282—enjoying some happy moments with Amit Shahji, J P Naddaji, Yogi Adityanathji and Ramlalji, after the strenuous election campaigns

Offering prayers to Sardar Patel and Swatantryaveer Savarkar, seeking knowledge, power and mental strength

Sevika forever: visual representation of everlasting *sanskars* of Rashtra Sevika Samiti

A traditional welcome by Governor of Manipur, Sushri Najma Heptulla

Friends forever : enjoying some true affectionate moments with late Sushma Swarajji

Loyal associates in the political journey—Late Arun Jaitleyji, late Ananth Kumarji and Shri Nitin Gadkariji

Brotherly conversation with Rajnath Singhji

Happy moments with the then President, late Shri Pranab Mukherjee

A moment of pride to deliver speech in Duma

With a Buddhist Monk at sanctuary in Mangolia

With Vice President
Shri Venkaiah Naiduji

At Suriratna memorial
in South Korea

A prestigious moment to be honoured with 'Mother of Speakers' by UNO

Launching of the Web Portal of Speaker's Research Initiative (SRI)

Paying tributes to Bharat Ratna Dr. Babasaheb Ambedkar

Accepting 'Padma Bhushan' award from
President Shri Ram Nath Kovindji

government took up the issue. Late Sushma Swaraj, as the Foreign Minister, made full preparations as she realised that for fixing the international boundaries, approval of the Parliament, Lok Sabha and Rajya Sabha was essential. The Bill was passed unanimously by 180 out of 180 votes in the Rajya Sabha On May 6-7, 2015. Later, Sushma Swaraj put it on the table in the Lok Sabha to be presented to *Taai*. [The Bharatiya Janata Party had earlier opposed the LBA (Land Boundary Agreement) but after coming to power, it changed its stand in the circumstances to control illegal infiltration.

After the creation of Bangladesh in 1971, and 41 years after the 1974 agreement, the Lok Sabha unanimously passed the Constitution (119th Amendment) Bill, a land boundary agreement exchanging territories between India and Bangladesh. The 331 members present voted in favour of the 100th Amendment. But it is necessary to mention an occasion which seems inconsistent. The only MP to oppose the bill, Sirajuddin Ajmal (All India United Democratic Front), urged the government to withdraw it and build a concrete wall around Bangladesh. According to him, Muslims in Assam had suffered for years and he opposed the Bill because they were discriminated against as Bangladeshis. However, he boycotted the vote and walked out of the House. The proposal was then put to a vote, and passed unanimously. With the exception of that, all party leaders spoke in favour of the proposal and voted in its favour. Prime Minister Modi himself rose from his seat and thanked the Opposition.

> *The esteemed newspaper, The Hindu also wholeheartedly praised it. Shrimati Smita Gupta wrote on May 7 that all the 331 members present in the House voted for the Bill which became the 100th Constitutional Amendment passed by Parliament.*
>
> *In a rare show of bi-partisanship, Parliament*

unanimously approved the Constitution (119th Amendment) Bill, operationalising the Land Boundary Agreement– swapping pf territories between India and Bangladesh– 41 years after the 1974 Indira Gandhi-Sheikh Mujibur Rehman pact.

The unity of purpose witnessed in the Rajya Sabha on Wednesday was repeated in the Lok Sabha on Thursday.

If External Affairs Minister Sushma Swaraj, who piloted the Bill, came in for praise from all sides of the House, Prime Minister Narendra Modi walked across the floor to thank Sonia Gandhi and Mallikarjun Kharge (Congress), Bhartuhan Mahtab (BJD), Sudip Bandopadhyay (Trinamool Congress) and P. Venugopal (AIADMK) for their support. He followed this up later, by phoning Bangladesh Prime Minister Sheikh Hasina and Chief Ministers of the five states affected by the Bill to thank them for their cooperation.

The Prime Minister of India, Narendra Modi and Prime Minister of Bangladesh, Sheikh Hasina signed the Land Boundary Agreement on June 6, 2015 at Dhaka in Bangladesh. From India, Bangladesh got 111 enclaves, adding up to 17,160,63 acres. India received 51 enclaves, adding up to 7.110.02 acres, from Bangladesh. The historic agreement made life easier for the common people.

Taai was satisfied that the issue had got streamlined. However, *Taai* says, "Those days were very disturbing; I was restless. It is important to note that in the land swap, Bangladesh gained more territory than India did. But the unforgivable procrastination of the previous rulers had caused endless miseries and persecution of the people of India and Bangladesh. Ratification of the land boundary agreement relieved the people from years of harassment; especially the people of Assam who were tormented due to discontent and

He signed the Instrument of Surrender in Dhaka on December 16, 1971, marking the formation of East Pakistan as the new nation of Bangladesh. Pakistan lost half pf its territory with the birth of Bangladesh.

Later, the Simla Agreement was signed between India and Pakistan and talks were held between Zulfikar Ali Bhutto, the President of Pakistan and Indira Gandhi, the Prime Minister of India. The agreement paved the way for diplomatic recognition of Bangladesh by Pakistan. But the Kashmir issue remained unresolved.

The agreement converted the ceasefire line of December 17, 1971 into the Line of Control (LOC) between India and Pakistan and it was agreed that "neither side will seek to alter it unilaterally, irrespective of mutual differences and legal interpretations." Experts believe that India missed the opportunity to convert the LOC into international border.

Having won the 1971 war, with so many prisoners of war in hand, our leaders failed to prove their astuteness in political negotiations. Hence, the golden opportunity to resolve the Kashmir issue permanently went astray. We won the battle indeed, however we lost in agreements and negotiations! It has caused a permanent sore in our minds just like a bleeding forehead of Ashvatthama, the great warrior in *Mahabharata*!

Later, Pakistan resorted to terrorism, instead of a direct war. All the border areas of Punjab, Kashmir and northeast India remained troubled.

Problems worsen if not attended on time. Greater losses have to be endured if prompt decisions are not made. One has to pay a heavy price for one's mistakes. Hence, politicians and administrators should be cautious, constantly vigilant and on their toes always. In the midst of all the circumstances, *Taai's* contribution in Lok Sabha to change the map of borders of India and Bangladesh is significant.

□

9

Her Icon, Ahilyabai

मुख्य सुत्र हाती घ्यावे।
करणे ते लोकांकरवी ठरवावे।
कित्येक खलक उगवावे।
राजकारणामधे॥

Mukhya sutra hati ghyave.
Karane te lokakaravi tharavave.
Kityeka khalaka ugavave.
Rajakaranamadhe.

(Dasbodh, 19.9.18)

(Control of the project should be kept in one's own hands and efforts should be made to see to get the project completed through others, while troublemakers are to be handled tactfully and with political acumen).

—Samarth Ramdas

After marriage, Sumitrataai came to the vibrant city of Indore and slowly got acquainted with its glorious history and culture. As Sumitratai was socially inclined right from the beginning, she got involved with many socio-cultural organisations in Indore – Devi Ahilya Utsav Committee was the foremost among them.

When Taai started working with Rashtra Sevika Samiti, she

was greatly fascinated by the personalities of Rani Ahilyadevi, Jijamata and Rani Jhansi and soon they became her role models.

People of Indore genuinely revered Devi Ahilyabai. Though Ahilyabai was a queen, people gave her a higher stature by addressing her as 'Mata' (mother). As *Taai* started reading more about the queen, she became more and more mesmerised by the many significant traits of her character. *Taai* was totally engrossed....Ahilyamata became her ideal... her inspiration in life. "Noble ruler who had rare social and political acumen Ahilyamata left so deep an impression on my mind that I did not even realise when simplicity, honesty, uprightness and dedication became my goals in social as well as political life. With unwavering faith in Ahilyamata, I accepted every challenge in life," Sumitratai points out.

With the purpose to immortalise the memories of the noble queen and to spread her ideals, the eminent personalities in Indore established the Ahilya Utsav Committee in 1915. *Taai's* association with Ahilya Utsav Committee started way back in 1981 and grew stronger and stronger over the years. Shrimati Sharayu Waghmare, Taai's long-time associate in the committee, throws light on Taai's connection and contributions to Ahilya Utsav Committee over four decades.

"Known for her simplicity, honesty and clean politics, *Taai* invoked great curiosity and respect in my mind. It is my good fortune that I got the chance to work with her and learn so many things from her," states Sharayutai.

Taai started joined the Devi Ahilya Utsav Committee as a volunteer in 1981. After handling many responsibilities, such as coordinator of women's convention, woman's representative and associate secretary, *Taai* became the president of the organisation in 1994.

Taai always maintained: "It is our responsibility to pass on the ideals that Devi Ahilyabai had set in her life to the next generation. That is why we try to remember her virtues and the noble work through various programmes."

Ever since *Taai* became the chairman of the committee, the programmes became more diverse and began to be celebrated on a grand scale.

The committee celebrated Ahilya Utsav annually on *Shravan Krishna Chaturdashi* (according to the Hindu calendar) to commemorate the death anniversary of the brave queen of Indore, Rani Ahilyabai. The image of the queen is worshiped in the morning and *aarti* is performed at the palace. The main function is performed at Gandhi Hall in the afternoon and the grand procession of the queen's palanquin is carried out in the evening with great enthusiasm. People of all castes and religions, various groups and even youth of the city enthusiastically join the procession, reciting *bhajans* and prayers. Bands, *akhade, jhanki, bhajan mandali,* youth dressed up like kings and emperors of the past, and 'women *sena*' on vibrantly decorated horses are the main attractions. The *shobha yatra* (procession) ends at Gopal Mandir. *Taai* always keeps a close eye on all the preparations.

Shrimati Sharayutai recalls her first meeting with *Taai,* "We had organised a *punyatithi* programme. The preparations were on. *Taai* arrived at the venue an hour earlier. While observing the arrangements, the expression on her face suddenly changed, "What is this? Why has no *rangoli* been drawn? Is it not an essential part in any cultural programme in India?" she asked.

"We realised our mistake. I learnt some lessons about planning and detailing and basic check-ups for any programme in the very first meeting with *Taai*. We learnt more and more as the years passed," Sharayutai adds.

The committee constituted Devi Ahilya Bai National Award on the 200th death anniversary of the warrior queen. Since 1996, the honour was bestowed on a person who worked at the national level as per the ideals of the queen. The award consists of a shawl, *shrifal* (coconut), citation and an honorarium of Rs. 1 lakh. *Taai* also introduced a novel practice regarding the award – the money for this reward is raised entirely from public contributions. The activists of the committee go door-to-door to collect the fund for the award from the common people. It not only helps to keep the memories of Devi Ahilyabai alive in people's mind but engenders a sense of belonging and pride that an eminent personality is being felicitated by the 'people'.

The first award was presented to social reformer, Nanaji Deshmukh by the then Prime Minister of the country, Atal Bihari Vajpayee and till now, twenty-one distinguished personalities have been honoured by celebrities.

The 221st Ahilya Utsav on 19 September, 2016 was one more memorable event. As a chief guest at the function, the then Governor of Uttar Pradesh, Ram Naik emphasised that working towards women empowerment, the socio-economic upliftment of the vulnerable and the spread of education among the masses would be a real homage to Rani Ahilyadevi. Her efficient system of government, formation of religious public trusts would always be inspiring in the future.

The committee decided to renovate the 60-year-old committee building under the guidance of *Taai*. The *bhoomi poojan* was performed on 19 October, 2017 by Hon'ble Union Minister Nitin Gadkari. Almost 75 per cent of the work has been completed; the rest of the work will be completed soon with the help of public support.

Taai also initiated many innovative programmes on cleanliness, preserving culture and women empowerment.

Indore has been ranked India's cleanest city under the Centre's annual cleanliness survey repeatedly for five times in a row. Taai always believed that people's awareness, their voluntary participation and cooperation are the key factors for any sustainable change. When Hon'ble

Prime Minister Narendra Modiji initiated the Swachh Bharat Abhiyan, Taai was instrumental in starting a novel initiative jointly with the Ahilya Utsav Committee and Mahanagar Vikas Parishad in Indore. A lot of effort has been made to clear the city from garbage and special vans were deployed to ensure that the city was kept clean. Taai put together teams in small localities and mohallas to go out and spread awareness regarding cleanliness. She also launched a drive to clean and decorate places of worship in the city before Diwali, just as we clean and decorate our homes to celebrate and welcome the festival.

Many of the camphor saplings that *Taai* received as gifts were planted in gardens around Indore. She also planted camphor and basil saplings in different parts of the city to reduce carbon footprints and provide clean oxygen to the people in and around the city. Committees were appointed for the conservation of seedlings.

Taai not only proposed unique ideas, but also paid attention towards their proper implementation. She is a perfectionist who believes in working out the smallest of details and regular follow-ups of plans. *Taai* has always celebrated her birthday by planting trees. She appointed a committee for each tree she planted. Each committee was required to measure how many inches the plant had grown and submit the report to Devi Ahilya Utsav Committee. The first-hand experience of working at the ground level and this sort of attention to minute details and follow-up helped her while working as a Speaker.

And while doing all this social work, she went beyond party politics. She always remained all-inclusive. Proper gradation of work, appointing appropriate people for the work, involving a suitable institution in the work to ensure smooth continuity of the work...*Taai* really excelled in work management.

It was due to her inspiration that a unique three-day Veda Lecture Festival was organised by Devi Ahilya Utsav Committee in the country. It attracted attention and increased curiosity of the general public towards the ancient texts.

When news of atrocities on women created fear in the society, *Taai* proposed to form the Ahilya Sena. She talked to young boys and girls in various areas and shaped a strong force of Ahilya Sena. Thus nobody even dared to mistreat a woman in the area!

Taai firmly believes, "Anyone, be it a woman or a man, who will follow in the footsteps of Goddess Ahilyamata will not victimise women and stand up against their mistreatment and the army of Ahilya will emerge automatically."Known for her wisdom and administrative skills, Ahilyabai Holkar is regarded as one of the finest female rulers in Indian history. On many occasions Ahilyabai led the army herself. As a ruler of Malwa kingdom, she spread the message of *dharma* and promoted industrialisation in the 18th century.

Taai imbibed qualities from Ahilyabai and these became useful at every stage of her life. *Taai* believed that the ideals of Ahilyabai are important in social work as well as in politics. That is why she strived hard to install a statue of Devi Ahilyabai in Parliament House.

This was indeed 'a dream come true' for *Taai* when on behalf of Ahilya Utsav Samiti on 24 August, 2006, the statue was unveiled by the then Vice President Bhairon Singh Shekhawat in the Parliament Library building.

Shrimati Sharyutai Waghmare expresses *Taai* emotions very aptly, "When *Taai* got permission to erect a statue of Ahilyabai in Parliament House, her enthusiasm knew no bounds. She invited models from reputed sculptors across the country, discussed with the experts, took their opinion and then selected the best model. When the statue was installed, tears of joy flowed from her eyes, endlessly.

"A bit of agony remained that the statue was a little behind. But installing a statue was not a mean task. It required some persistent efforts. When *Taai* was the Minister of State, she made a suggestion to the then Speaker of the Lok Sabha, Manohar Joshi. The suggestion then went to a special committee for the erection of statues and photographs for approval. Speaker Manohar Joshi was Chairperson of that committee. He approved *Taai's* suggestion/application then and there. It got through due to his prompt support.

However, by then, the BJP and allied parties had lost power in the Centre. Taai was no more a minister but just an MP. But when *Taai* decides on something, she leaves no stone unturned to fulfill it. She continuously pursued the matter. In the end, the implementation was done by the then Speaker of the Lok Sabha, Somnath Chatterjee," Sharayutai adds.

And thus a bronze statue of Devi Ahilyabai Holkar, the 18th-century ruler of Malwa, was installed in the Parliament Library building. The 75 1/2 inch statue, carved by sculptor Shashikant Varke, was donated by Sumitra Mahajan, MP, on behalf of Ahilya Utsav Samiti, Indore. The statue was unveiled by Vice-President Bhairon Singh Shekhawat in the presence of Prime Minister Manmohan Singh. Floral tributes were paid to Ahilyabai by the dignitaries which included UPA Chairperson, Sonia Gandhi, Defence Minister Pranab Mukherjee, BJP leader L.K. Advani, many Cabinet ministers and MPs. When *Taai* became the Speaker of the Lok Sabha, she had the opportunity to reinstall the same statue in the Parliament Library. What a great honour it was to have an idol of such a great ruler reinstalled at a prominent place in the Lok Sabha!

...Subhedar Malharrao Holkar was the first Maratha Governor of Malwa and a great follower of Shivaji Maharaj, He also was a special Sardar-Subhedar of the first Bajirao Peshwa, who did not lose a single battle and expanded the Hindu empire all over India. (Shinde, Holkar, Gaekwad are the main pillars of the Maratha empire, in North India). Ahilyabai was his daughter-in-law. Malhar

Baba recognised her virtues and trained her to be a prudent ruler. After the demise of Malhar Baba, Ahilyabai became the ruler of Malwa. Due to her fair policies and prudent financial management of the state, this period is considered as the golden age of Malwa.

The journal of parliamentary information states:

New Delhi, 11 April, 2017:

Prime Minister Shri Narendra Modi released a book Matoshree authored by Lok Sabha Speaker Smt. Sumitra Mahajan in Parliament Library Building (PLB). The book covers the life and times of Devi Ahilyabai Holkar. After the release of the book, a play based on the book was staged in GMC Balayogi Auditorium, PLB and was watched by Prime Minister, several Union Ministers, Members of Parliament and other invitees. The play Matoshree was divided into 15 scenes wherein the author Smt. Sumitra Mahajan has, with great sensitivity and understanding, depicted the struggles, predicaments and qualities of Devi Ahilyabai Holkar right from the time when she became a daughter-in-law of Subedar Malhar Rao Holkar. The play was a unique blend of all the elements of theatre, which not only made the play a visual delight for the viewers but also inspired the artistes and performers with its intrinsic message. The play was organised by Avirat and was directed by Rajan Deshmukh.

In fact, Sumitrataai had written the play more than 35 years ago, as a volunteer of the Rashtra Sevika Samiti, women's wing of the RSS. Around 1984, senior sevikas of Rashtra Sevika Samiti, such as Malati Taai Waghmare and Vatsalataai Namjoshi and others thought of staging plays on the three role models of the Samiti – Rani Lakshmibai, Mata Jijabai and Punyashlok Ahilyabai. Plays had already been performed on Mata Jijabai and Rani Lakshmibai. The responsibility of writing a play on Ahilyabai with thorough study was given to Taai. Taai had never written a play before, but, perhaps, Taai had inherited her father's love for theatre. (Her father had directed and performed 22 plays in Chiplun between 1920 and 1950).

Malatitaai was confident that Taai could do it. The first rehearsal of the play was decided, but Taai had not even completed the first act of the play. But, if Taai is given any responsibility, she completes the work, come what may!

Taai writes in the preface of the book, Matoshree: "I reached home, thinking. Whenever there is a problem, I remember my gurudev Nana Maharaj Taranekar. Recalling my guru, I sat down to write. The first act was completed. Everyone liked it the next day. The same process continued for some days. Scene by scene the play was progressing. This is how the play was completed. On the occasion of the reinstallation of the statue of Goddess Ahilyamata at a new place, people of Indore got hold of the old script of the play, revived it and presented it beautifully.

Due to this, Taai's name was recorded as a writer in 'Kaun Banega Crorepati'.

There was a question in the first episode of the 12th season of the popular show in Hindi in television.

Answer the following question:

'Matoshree is a book written by former Lok Sabha Speaker Sumitra Mahajan.

The book is based on the life of which Indian queen?'

(a) Rani Lakshmibai
(b) Rani Padmini
(c) Rani Durgavati
(d) Rani Ahilyabai Holkar

The answer is: 'Rani Ahilyabai Holkar'

More than 1,200 people from Indore went to Parliament for the memorable programme. People tried to reach the venue by whichever transport was available and at their own expenses, out of love and respect for Devi Ahilyamata and *Taai.*

Taai was showered with accolades. However, she modestly attributed all the credit to her ideal, Mata Ahilyadevi. On the occasion, *Taai's* humble words are quite eloquent, "The play, written about 35 years ago, was in the form of a manuscript. Vitthalrao Gawde of Ahilya Utsav Committee wanted to publish this book but I was not convinced because, first of all, I am not a writer and this was a historical drama, thus it was important to verify the facts minutely. It could have had discrepancies. I was hesitant. What if something went wrong? But this responsibility was taken over by Sharad Pagare, noted historian and an expert on Ahilyabai; he re-edited the book and got it printed.

"While discussing with Prime Minister Narendra Modi, the idea came up to reinstall the statue of Goddess Ahilyamata at a prominent place so that it could be visible to all. Prabhat Prakashan then agreed to print the book. Artistes from Indore expressed their desire to perform the play. The event was planned. Still I was a little hesitant to publish the book. When I went to Prime Minister Modi to invite him to the event and to see the play, the subject of the book and the publication came forward. The Prime Minister readily agreed to attend the event and get the book published. I had a clear idea that I got this approval not because I am a writer but because of the virtue of Goddess Ahilyabai, because the person on whom this book is based is exemplary. The figure in this artwork is brilliant. The protagonist of the play is universal, supreme, all-pervasive and omnipresent even today. That is why this book titled *Matoshree* is a tribute to Ahilyamata."

The review of the play is also very eloquent. Matoshree *is a dramatic presentation of the character who truly became a mother of the people. The author has written it, inspired by Goddess Ahilyabai. The play has a deep and lasting effect due to its effective presentation. Sumitraji is not a writer but her devotion to Goddess Ahilyabai has made her a great playwright. The play* Matoshree *portrays the great virtues of motherhood of Goddess Ahilyabai.*

The play is not just a delight to read but it is a unique blend of all the elements of theatre that has made the play a visual delight for the viewers as well. The tone, language, dialogues and characters are effective. The author has given a unique expression to the tragic personal life of Matoshree Ahilyabai through the play. It is indeed an all-time inspiring play. The event became memorable for yet another awesome gesture. After releasing the book, Matoshree, *the Prime Minister kept the wrapper in his pocket instead of throwing it out.*

It was indeed a great homage to the clean, fair and just rule of Queen Ahilyabai who turned Malwa into a prosperous land, starting by improving the infrastructure of the place by building forts and roads, repairing and cleaning *ghats*; who built wells, tanks and rest-houses across areas stretching from the Himalayas to pilgrimage centres in South India; who sponsored festivals and gave donations to build, repair and restore temples (even from private funds). From Badrinath, Dwarka, Omkareshwar, Puri, Gaya, Rameswaram, every holy pilgrimage place in India made a contribution in one way or another, from Ahilyabai Holkar; who broke the old traditions and established the new ones; who believed in empowerment of women and giving equal property rights to women.

Now, the statue of Devi Ahilyamata in Parliament has become a great photo point. Scholars, observers and guests within the country and abroad make it a point to visit the place and feel blessed to take a photograph near the statue.

□

Book release of 'Matoshree' written by hon'ble Sumitrataai Mahajan	
https://www.youtube.com/watch?v=-cvTySEqWrc	

10

The Master Move

दीर्घ सूचना आयी कळे।
सावधपणे तर्क प्रबळे।
जाणजाणोनी निवळे।
येथा योग्य॥

Deergha Suchanaa aayee kaleI.
Savadhpane tark prabale.
JaaNJaanoni Nivale.
Yethaa Yogya.

(Dasbodh, 11.6.6)

(Such a leader understands indications and has foresight of things to come with alertness, the power of reasoning becomes strengthened, and many things are understood properly by persistently thinking them over. He has vision and clarity of thoughts.)

—Samarth Ramdas

The day was an important day for the Government and people of India. The Minister of Finance Arun Jaitley spoke: "Madam Speaker, I rise to move for leave to introduce a Bill to provide for, as a good governance, efficient, transparent, and targeted delivery of subsidies, benefits and services, the expenditure for which is incurred from the Consolidated Fund of India, to individuals residing in India through assigning of unique identity numbers to such individuals and for matters connected therewith or incidental thereto...."

(Interruptions)

Hon. Speaker: "I have allowed him."

(Interruptions)

Jyotiraditya Scindia (Guna): "Yes madam, but the fact is that it was introduced earlier by the UPA government. It had gone to the Standing Committee. Various recommendations had come in. It must not be introduced as the Money Bill."

Hon. Speaker: "He is introducing the Bill."

(Interruptions)

Jyotiraditya Scindia: "It must go to both the Houses of Parliament, Madam, 92 crore people are involved."

(Interruptions)

Hon. Speaker: "But today he is introducing only."

N.K. Premachandran (Kollam): "It should go to the Standing Committee. It was not even listed in the BAC also."

(Interruptions)

Hon. Speaker: "He is introducing only."

Jyotiraditya Scindia: "Madam, the fact is that it is being introduced as a Money Bill. It should be introduced as regular Finance Bill."

(Interruptions)

Hon. Speaker: "He is introducing it."

Jyotiraditya Scindia: "But, madam, we have an objection to the introduction of the Bill. (Interruptions)

Hon. Speaker: "But, he is only introducing it."

(Interruptions)

Hon. Speaker: "I do not understand it. You are not cooperating in introducing the Bill. (Interruptions)

Mallikarjun Kharge (Gulbarga): "We are ready to cooperate with that Bill but he should not introduce it as a Money Bill."

Hon. Speaker: "But he has just introduced it."

(Interruptions)

Mallikarjun Kharge: "To avoid Rajya Sabha, the government is taking it as a Money Bill." (Interruptions)

Hon. Speaker: "The question is that leave be granted to introduce the Bill to provide for, as a good governance, efficient, transparent and targeted delivery of subsidies, benefits and services, the expenditure for which is incurred from the Consolidated Fund of India, to individuals residing in India through assigning of unique identity numbers to such individuals and formatters connected therewith or incidental thereto."

The motion was adopted

Arun Jaitley: "Madam, I introduce the Bill - Aadhaar (Targeted Delivery of Financial and Other Subsidies, Benefits and Services) Bill, 2016."

Hon. Speaker: "The motion has been adopted. I have given the permission to the hon'ble minister to introduce the Bill."

Aadhaar bill was presented in Lok Sabha amid strong protests from Opposition members. *Taai* was determined and composed. There were arguments and counterarguments. However, she maintained her poise, gave everyone a chance to speak and successfully presented the Bill as Money Bill.

Before allowing the Bill to be presented in Lok Sabha, *Taai* thoroughly studied the matter.

Then Finance Minister Arun Jaitley solved all her queries and explained everything to her in detail. *Taai* never shied away from asking minute details and doubts and was always prepared to learn anything new. Though she was an experienced MP but she was not an expert in financial matters. She did not consider it below her dignity to accept the fact and was always willing to learn. Thus *Taai* thoroughly studied the background of the Aadhaar issue.

After the Kargil war, a committee was formed to study the state of national security. The committee recommended that citizens in border regions be issued identity cards on a priority basis.

The need for modernising payment systems in banks was first highlighted in the 2001 Vision Document of RBI.

In 2005, the RBI revisited the idea and put out the Vision Document II after studying payment systems in the US, UK., Europe, Japan, Singapore and China. It stated that the mission was "the establishment of safe, secure, sound and efficient payment and settlement systems for the country."

In 2008, post legislation and guidelines, an entity to do this was finally cleared. Later the Planning Commission notified UIDAI in January 2009.

The promise of unique identity was first outlined in the economic survey of 2009.

The 13th Finance Commission, chaired by Vijay Kelkar, proposed to pay Rs. 100 per person to all people below the poverty line and to create a grant of Rs. 29.89 billion for state governments.

At the 55th National Development Council meeting on July 24, 2010, Prime Minister Manmohan Singh presented the unique identity programme as an instrument to reduce fiscal deficit and deliver succour to the poor. "The operationalisation of the Unique Identification Number Scheme, together with developments in information technology, provide an opportunity to target subsidies effectively to those who really need them and deserve them."

At an interaction with newspaper editors, he said, "We need system reforms. If the UIDAI can give unique ID numbers to all our residents, we would have discovered a new pathway to eliminate the scope for corruption and leakages in distribution of subsidies."

The Reserve Bank of India held discussions with NABARD

and other concerned organisations on Aadhaar-based financial inclusion. In December 2010, then Finance Minister Pranab Mukherjee supported the Aadhaar project and said that it would be regarded as a valid document for opening bank account for Kisan Kalyan Yojana (KKY).

Meanwhile, Nandan Nilekani and his core team were reading a library of solutions– internally referred to as sleeper cells– for, as and when and if, a problem arose. Thus a problem can be spotted before it morphs into a full-fledged crisis and solutions could be worked out. This is because no problem is really new or has not been discussed in the system and documentation creates an opening, like in a chess game, for the next move.

The preparations were on. The main hurdle was how to link Aadhaar and bank account? Nearly two-third of Indians did not have bank accounts. The problem had two facets: access to banking and access to banks. Access to banking was haunted by poor processes– a primary cause being lack of documents for identification. Opening an account in banks was a complicated process, even making provision for minimum balance while opening an account was difficult for many. Access to banks was essentially hampered by the fact there were not enough bank branches. India had a total of 83,997 branches. Only 32,289 branches were giving services to more than 600,000 villages in India and nearly 6,000 cities were served by 51,708 branches.

The expected beneficiaries of government schemes were living in rural areas. Reaching out to them was a great challenge.

The positive aspect was the massive expansion of mobile phone subscription across India. In 2010, India's population was 1,210 million. Of these, less than a fourth had a bank account. Although the official score was over 600 million accounts, unique individual bank accounts were estimated to be around 250 million. India had 635.5 million mobile phone subscribers. Thus mobile service had much wider and deeper reach. It was realised that Aadhaar number could be linked to mobile and mobile to banks

In April 2010, the government approved a framework for providing financial services through mobile phones – through a mobile-based PIN system using 'Mobile Banking POS' and through a fingerprint-based system using Aadhaar numbers.

In September 2010, the government introduced Aadhaar scheme on an experimental basis in some rural areas of Maharashtra.

On December 3, 2010, the National Identification Authority of India Bill, 2010 (NIAI Bill) was introduced in Rajya Sabha by the UPA government.

On December 10, 2010, the NIAI Bill 2010 was referred by the Lok Sabha Speaker to a Standing Committee for examination and a report thereafter.

In December, 2011, the Standing Committee on Finance under Yashwant Sinha issued a report on the NIAI Bill and rejected the Bill in its initial form. It gave recommendations, including the requirement for an over-arching privacy legislation and data protection law before the continuance of the scheme, and expressed concern about private agencies being contracted for the collection of sensitive information.

On February 7, 2012, the UIDAI launched an online verification system for Aadhaar numbers. On November 26, the then Prime Minister Dr. Manmohan Singh launched a direct cash transfer scheme which would be linked with Aadhaar.

On November 30, 2012, Justice K.S. Puttaswamy, former Karnataka High Court Judge, filed a petition before the Supreme Court contending that Aadhaar does not have any statutory basis and moreover violates the fundamental nights of equality and privacy granted to every individual under the constitution.

On January 1, 2013, the government implemented Aadhaar-enabled service delivery initiative in 51 districts across the country. On September 23, the Supreme Court in its order said that some areas had issued circulars making Aadhaar mandatory, but no person should suffer if he does not have an Aadhaar card. National Payment Corporation of India (NPCI) launched Aadhaar-based payment system on October 9. However, the Aadhaar scheme was considered baseless due to lack of legal sanction.

Arun Jaitley was an economist and also a lawyer! In 2014, when he became the Finance Minister, he started all the preparations for re-enactment of the Bill. After making all the preparations, he presented Aadhaar (targeted delivery of financial and other subsidies, benefits and services) Bill, 2016 in the Lok Sabha.

But the question that remains unanswered is: 'The need to issue Aadhaar identity cards was realised and understood by both the National Democratic Alliance (NDA) BJP and its allies and the United Progressive Alliance (UPA) Congress and its allies in India, then why an appropriate collective stand was not taken while introducing the Bill? Was it a game of party politics, selfish manipulations?

Taai says many of the amendments suggested in the 2010 Bill were incorporated into the 2016 Bill. "However, the ruling party was skeptical about the approval of the Opposition – the Congress party then. The ruling party had a majority in the Lok Sabha but the Opposition parties had an upper hand in the Rajya Sabha. I realised that if the Bill is ad hoc, then the concessions and services would not be provided to the general public in a transparent manner and corruption would not be controlled. My conscience gave a nod to find a way out."

According to the electoral system of Indian democracy, the Lok Sabha is dissolved before the General

Elections, which means that all members lose the right to act as MPs. After re-election of Lok Sabha, the new Lok Sabha is formed by the elected members. That is why we call the Lok Sabha, from 2014 to 2019, as the 16th Lok Sabha. But the Rajya Sabha is never dissolved. Every six years, one-third, or about 80 members, retire and are replaced by new members. This is a continuous process and having a majority in the Lok Sabha does not mean having a majority in the Rajya Sabha. This is a distinct feature of the Indian Constitution. Therefore, both the Houses have control over each other.

The Bill was introduced by the Congress-led government in 2010. Later, the Standing Committee made some recommendations and suggested changes. A brief comparison of the provisions (clauses) of the 2016 and 2010 Bills is as follows:

No.	Provisions	2016	2010
1.	Who is entitled?	Any person who has resided in India for 182 days before registration	Any person residing in India
2.	Use	To receive a government subsidy or service	No such provision
3.	Verification	It will not confer any right of citizenship	Similar provision
4.	Information required	Biometric and demographic photo	Biometric and photo not specified
5.	Purpose	Concessions and providing service	Purpose is not mentioned
6.	Enrolment and authentication	Right to access information	No such provision
7.	Time period	Information could be seen repeatedly	Time period not specified

8.	System to analyse	Does not have any system to analyse and no Identity Review Committee	Identity Review Committee can analyse data anytime across the country
9.	Restrictions on sharing information	Information cannot be shared for other purposes	No such provision
10.	Oversight committee	Details relation between national security committee and Aadhaar and guiding principles	No requirement for any committee
11.	Role of courts	Demographic information would be provided only on court orders	Had a similar clause
12.	Offences and penalties	A person will be imprisoned for up to three years and fine of not less than Rs.10 lakh	Imprisonment for three years and the fine of Rs. 1 crore
13.	Penalties	Defalcation of funds by enrolling agency-fine of Rs. 1 lakh	No such provision.

After *Taai* had studied all the minute details and was convinced that the Bill could be presented in Parliament, she gave her consent. Actually it is the responsibility of the Speaker to manage the smooth functioning of Lok Sabha. So *Taai* had to be fully convinced. Taai had set some guidelines for herself.

The examination of Articles 107 to 117 of the constitution indicates the following kinds of Bills:

i. General Bills (Article 107)
ii. Money Bills (Article 110)
iii. Appropriation Bills (Article 114)
iv. Financial Bills (Article 117)

Aadhaar Bill was to be presented as Financial Bill. The Bill was first introduced as the National Identification Authority of India (NIDAI) Bill in the Upper House of Parliament on December 3, 2010 by the UPA government. A week later, it was referred by the Lok Sabha Speaker to the Standing Committee on Finance, but it could not become a law. A lot of time had already been wasted. If history was repeated, then an important initiative would have suffered a great setback and the common people would have been deprived of its benefits. Thus, the government presented the Bill as Money Bill (Article-110).

> *A Money Bill can be introduced only in Lok Sabha and not in Rajya Sabha. On the question whether a Bill is a Money Bill or not, the decision of the Speaker is final.*
>
> *On every Money Bill, Speaker endorses a certificate signed by him/her to the effect that it is a Money Bill, before the Bill is sent to Rajya Sabha or presented to the President for approval.*

On March 3, 2016, the Aadhaar Bill, 2016 was introduced in Parliament as a Money Bill by Finance Minister Arun Jaitley. The Opposition parties tried hard to put up a united protest to the government's move. *Taai's* moderate policy and skill to handle the situation patiently helped to conduct smooth proceedings.

The decision to introduce it as a Money Bill was criticised by the Opposition parties. Ghulam Nabi Azad, an INC leader, wrote in a letter to Arun Jaitley that the ruling party, BJP, was trying to bypass the Rajya Sabha, as they did not have the majority in the Upper House.

Jyotiraditya Scindia of INC asked why a new Bill was introduced when the National Identification Authority of India Bill, 2010 was still pending in the Rajya Sabha.

The Bill was passed on March 11, 2016 by the Lok Sabha by a voice vote after a brief debate.

The use of Aadhaar cards would curtail malpractices worth crores of rupees on social schemes. In the year 2016, the government will have full emphasis on this. By making Aadhaar mandatory, the government can curb leakages up to Rs. 50,000 to Rs. 70,000 crore annually.

Currently, the government spends nearly Rs. 3.5 lakh crore on various social welfare schemes in the country. The government believes that benefits through these schemes would start reaching the poor from the next financial year. Once the Bill is approved by the President, the government will allow the use of Aadhaar card in banking, tax and service sectors. Also mobile connection for Aadhaar card can be taken.

Tathagata Satpathy of Biju Janata Dal (BJD) had expressed concern that the project could be used for mass surveillance or ethnic cleansing in future. He also raised questions about why a new identity card project was created despite having several identity card systems. He also questioned why the Bill was introduced as a Money Bill and also why, when the Bill allows sharing of biometric under the circumstances of national security, no concrete definition of national security was included.

Bhartruhari Mahtab of BJD requested that the Bill should not be rushed and referred to a parliamentary panel. Mallikarjun Kharge of INC said that they supported the Bill but wanted some suggestions to be discussed. Rajeev Satav of INC reminded the House that initially the ruling-party BJP had opposed the Aadhaar during the reign of United Progressive Alliance (UPA) and had now turned around and supported it.

During the debate, Finance Minister Arun Jaitley assured

the House that the Aadhaar project will not be misused. He stated that 97% of adults and 67% of children had already been registered under the project. He also said that the definition of national security was up to the courts to define. (It was later defined by the courts)

On March 15, 2016, the Bill came forward in the Rajya Sabha for discussion. Shumsher K. Sheriff, Secretary of the Rajya Sabha, formally notified the House that the Bill had been passed in the Lok Sabha. During the debate spanning over two days, Naresh Agrawal of Samajwadi Party (SP) said that the Bill doesn't fit into the definition of a Money Bill. P.J. Kurien, Deputy Chairman of Rajya Sabha, said that it was the decision of Lok Sabha Chairperson, Sumitra Mahajan, to allow the Bill, so it should not be questioned. Sitaram Yechury of Communist Party of India (Marxist) (CPI-M) argued that the Bill was unconstitutional as the constitution guarantees the freedom of life and liberty and privacy came under it.

Arun Jaitley responded to Yechury by saying that privacy is not an absolute right and it can be restricted by the law.

Jairam Ramesh of INC said Aadhaar should be limited to subsidies only and not made mandatory for any purpose.

On March 15, 2016, the Bill was returned to the Lok Sabha by the Rajya Sabha with some suggested amendments. The Lok Sabha was free to accept or reject the amendments. Lok Sabha rejected the amendments and passed the Bill.

On May 10, 2016, Congress leader Jairam Ramesh challenged the passing of the Aadhaar Act as a Money Bill. The Supreme Court rejected his plea and said the decision was valid as the expenditure for the benefits under the scheme would come out of the Consolidated Fund of India. On September 14, the court ruled that it was wrong to make Aadhaar mandatory for scholarships.

On January 5, 2017, the court ruled that it was not appropriate to assign the responsibility of data collection to a private company. The Aadhaar linking deadline was extended from December 15 to March 31, 2018. In March 2017, the government added a new Section 139-AA to the Income-tax Act and made Aadhaar mandatory for filing income-tax returns along with PAN card. The JAM initiative then linked the Jan Dhan Yojana's bank account number, Aadhaar number and mobile number to provide direct and personal benefits to the poor and needy. In a way, it was an economic and social revolution.

On January 17, 2017, the five-judge bench started hearing the Aadhaar case. On March 7, the bench said that Aadhaar could not be mandatory for national-level entrance examinations, such as NEET and other examinations. The court had reserved judgment in this case. The court delivered its verdict on September 26. Thus, the limits of the use of Aadhaar were fixed. The court gave the verdict that Aadhaar was not required for academic admission, but Aadhaar was required if one wanted to benefit from scholarships or other educational schemes.

Today we are experiencing the benefits of Aadhaar. Similarities are often drawn between politics and chess. Like chess players, politicians need to be confident and decide the moves intelligently and cautiously. They have to make strategic choices within the constraints of a map– right move at the right time.

The unique jump over of two-and-a-half squares by the knight proved effective in Parliament. Indeed, the tricky piece stunned the opponents and provided Aadhaar and relief to the needy.

□

11

SRI–Initiating New Concepts

वेदशास्त्रीं सत्य स्वरूप।
तेंचि ज्ञानियांचे रूप।
पुण्य जालें अमूप।
सुकृतें सीमा सांडिली॥

Vedashastri satyaswarupa.
Techi Dnyaniyanche rupa.
Punya jale amupa.
Sukrute seema sandali.

(Dasbodh, 10.10.66)

(The Vedas and other scriptures describe the true nature of Truth and that itself is the form of the Creator whose virtues are immeasurable and whose good deeds are limitless.)

—Samarth Ramdas

The Speakers Research Initiative (SRI)– Adhyaksha Shodh Kadam (ASHOK)– is one of the most important and wonderful initiatives not only in the 16th Lok Sabha but also in the history of Indian Parliament.

Based on her long experience in parliamentary and public life, Sumitra Mahajan decided to establish SRI, her brainchild to be inaugurated by Prime Minister Narendra Modi on July 23, 2015.

The Members of Parliament had to discuss an array of diversified subjects. In today's world of super specialisation, it is difficult for every Member of Parliament to have a deep knowledge on a variety of subjects. SRI provides a platform where Members of Parliament can interact with domain experts and benefit from their expertise.

Parliaments and legislatures in the world are faced continuously with new challenges. They have to respond to these emerging challenges, make laws and exercise oversight over a plethora of issues, both internal and external, that keep getting more complex by the day. In order to do justice to their supremely important responsibilities, it is imperative that members of legislative bodies are empowered with proper understanding of these issues and their implications. Informed legislators can always make wise, relevant and effective laws and policies as well as exercise effective oversight over the executive. The need for such a forum like SRI is all the more important as new Members in the Parliament get an opportunity to interact with domain experts and their peers. It was felt that apart from the research that is made available to the members, mechanisms for a deeper and wider understanding of issues were required. With this objective, eminent experts from diverse disciplines were brought together by Hon'ble Speaker Sumitra Mahajan to devise mechanisms for the benefit of Members of Parliament. The group came up with the idea of workshops focusing on important issues where eminent experts and Members of Parliament could interact with each other in a face-to-face dialogue. This combination of two perspectives of the MPs equipped with a real grasp of the reality on the ground in their respective constituencies and of the experts with strong academic knowledge creates an effective mechanism for knowledge sharing and capacity building.

SRI, that began in 2015, had nine members. Its objectives included:

1. Identify major areas/issues of long term, strategic policy significance as well as of topical importance.
2. Generate high-quality research inputs and make available latest critical knowledge and expertise to members of both the Houses of Parliament for information dissemination, knowledge sharing and capacity building.
3. Devise interactive, participatory mechanisms for effective knowledge sharing amongst the members and experts.

Key activities of SRI cover the following five broad areas:

1. Workshops for MPs on issues of national/ international importance.
2. Meetings of subject-specific SRI groups.
3. Events like conferences, seminars, round-table discussions, etc.
4. The internship scheme.
5. The fellowship scheme.

The SRI groups concentrate mainly on seven subjects:

1. Agriculture
2. Education
3. Health
4. Environment and Climate Change
5. Women and Child Development
6. Finance
7. Infrastructure and Housing

So far, more than 80 MPs from Rajya Sabha and Lok Sabha have become the members of these groups. The Members of Parliament are aware of the real problems of people and the experts have the technical knowledge on the subject; thus it benefits both.

Workshops

Since its inception, SRI has held 32 workshops on important issues, invited a number of distinguished experts on these issues and provided several publications, backgrounders and reports to MPs. Through these, SRI has been able to generate a high degree of awareness and interest among the Members of Parliament and other legislators. It has augmented and expanded their understanding of issues of national and international importance. An overwhelming number of Members of Parliament from both the Houses, including ministers, have participated in and benefited from these activities. It is a common platform extended to both the members of Rajya Sabha (Council of States) and Lok Sabha (House of the People). Some of the major issues on which SRI has organised workshops so far are Sustainable Development Goals (SDGs), Goods and Services Tax (GST), Unorganised Sector, Water Management, Drought and Interlinking of Rivers, Agriculture, Health, Education, Constitution of India, Simultaneous Elections, Neo-Protectionism in International Trade, Internal Security and India's Start-up Phenomena, etc.

I am an indirect witness of the initiative. Being a researcher myself, I took great interest in research work. Sometimes I got information about these subjects from Dr. Kirit Somaiya. I remember, nearly 1,200 applications were received for 100 seats. It reveals that positive-minded youngsters of the country were interested in learning about democracy and related subjects. Taai's efforts received a tremendous response.

Internship

In the 16th Lok Sabha for the first time more than 300 Members of Parliament were elected. They needed the helpful information and the assistants who could provide it. Thus,

Taai added Lok Sabha Internship Programme in SRI. The Internship Scheme is aimed at providing an opportunity to the students with excellent academic credentials to acquaint themselves with the working of parliamentary democracy and parliamentary procedures and to train them to contribute towards generation of research inputs for Members of Parliament. Two batches of 25 interns, each of one month and three months, were decided. Candidates received apprenticeship for one-month internship. Everyone submitted their digital and typed research essays. The response to the SRI initiative was overwhelming. Various Members of Parliament have said in their comments that it had helped them to be active and positive participants in debates of Parliament and the quality of discussion also increased.

The successful use of SRI was appreciated by Inter Parliamentary Union (IPU) and Commonwealth Parliamentary Association (CPA). Not only India's neighboring countries but also developed countries showed interest to participate in the initiative.

In addition, SRI has organised 37 workshops and seminars, focusing on organic farming, education, health, internal security, seven development goals, etc. and helped and also increased the quality level of discussion.

The successful use of SRI has been well-known in the Inter Parliamentary Union (IPU) and in the international arena. It was also heard in the Commonwealth Parliamentary Association (CPA) and was much appreciated by the people. In addition to our verticals, many developed countries also expressed their desire to join and take advantage of this initiative. SRI has not only organised seminars and workshops, but also a number of conferences.

Fellowship

In 2018-19, the Lok Sabha Secretariat under SRI awarded

research scholarships for high quality research on topics relevant to parliamentary democracy. Applications were invited for 25 posts of researchers for a period of two years. It was provided to encourage and support the original study on Indian parliamentary-related topics. Elected scholars had an open door in the Lok Sabha. *Taai* discussed with them, resolved their doubts and arranged their interactions with scholars on various subjects. She believed that the next generation should be properly trained for a healthy democracy.

Dr. Kirit Somaiya worked for the committee. He says, "SRI is Sumitrataai's unique contribution. It strengthens the parliamentary system, along with bringing together all sections of society– students, MPs, minsters, officials, professionals and teachers– to discuss various issues and hold workshops and conferences. She participated in every aspect, pursued the issues and remained connected. She suggested to all on how they could contribute to the development of the country. She encouraged them constantly. From my own experience, I can certainly say that *Taai* gave me the opportunity to participate in SRI and that is why I could study more. It contributed to my personal growth and increased my participation in contributing to the development of the country."

Such initiatives clearly show how *Taai* was always with times or perhaps ahead of times.

□

12
Honouring Constitution Day

जो एकांतास तत्पर।
आधी करी पाठांतर।
अथवा शोधी अर्थांतर।
ग्रंथगर्भीचे॥

Jo ekantasa tatpara.
Adhi kari Pathantara.
Athava shodhi arthantara.
Granthagarbhiche.

(Dasbodh, 11.6.9)

(He is eager to sit in solitude, he learns the important texts by heart and delves deep to find the hidden meanings of the texts.)

—Samarth Ramdas

Taai initiated many innovative ideas during her tenure as Speaker of 16th Lok Sabha. In 2015, the Government of India decided to celebrate November 26 as 'Constitution Day' to promote values of the constitution among citizens. *Taai* played an important role in the decision. Since then, the day is celebrated as Constitution Day; earlier it was known as National Law Day and was not celebrated in public.

Constitution Day, also known as 'Samvidhan Divas', is

celebrated in our country on November 26 every year to commemorate the adoption of the Constitution of India. On November 26, 1949, the Constituent Assembly of India adopted the Constitution of India, which came into effect from January 26, 1950. The day is also celebrated in memory of Dr. Bhimrao Ambedkar, who was the first Law Minister and also the first Chairman of the Drafting Committee that drafted the Constitution of India, one of the longest written constitutions of the world. The Drafting Committee took 2 years 11 months and 18 days to prepare the constitution.

The first Constitution Day was celebrated on November 26, 2015 at Vigyan Bhavan, Delhi. *Taai* was the chief guest. The speech delivered by *Taai* on the occasion gives a glimpse of her oratory skills. *Taai* is extremely careful while writing speeches and makes precise use of words. *Taai* prepared the speech with the help of her assistants. The scholarly pursuits are quite evident in the speech. The speech also reveals *Taai's* philosophy behind the work and commitment to achieve the objective. The word that was extremely important for her was '*hum*' and not 'I' or 'me'. This stressed the point that 'what we are trying to achieve is not for an individual but for everyone and together we have to achieve'.

According to *Taai*, this required some honest, sincere and loyal people. It also requires sacrifice; everyone should be aware of this. In addition to what we have achieved, *Taai* reminds us of where we have fallen short. "Women are under-represented in the political arena and competent women should be consciously brought into the arena," she maintained and *Taai* worked hard towards the goal.

Here is the famous speech by Hon'ble Speaker Sumitra Mahajan on November 26, 2018 that reveals her sharp, serious, scholarly and philosophical mind. The speech, available on the Lok Sabha Speaker's website, is originally in Hindi and here we present it in the translated form:

1. I am happy to participate in a discussion on 'Critical Analysis of the Achievement of the Country in the Light of Constitutional Expectations' organised by the Supreme Court of India to celebrate Constitution Day.
2. Friends! It is a matter of great joy for every citizen that our country has reached the milestone of 70 years of successful implementation of the constitution. We all know that after Independence, the Indian Constitution, which was drafted by the Special Constitutional Drafting Committee, was adopted on 26th November, 1949. To commemorate this, this day is being celebrated as Constitution Day. While preparing our constitution, the Chairman of the Drafting Committee of the constitution, Dr. Babasaheb Ambedkar and other prominent members and president of the Constituent Assembly, Dr. Rajendra Prasad, Pandit Jawaharlal Nehru, Sardar Vallabhbhai Patel, Dr. Syama Prasad Mookerjee and Mrs. Sucheta Kripalani and many others have made significant contributions. This day is a tribute to the nation for their erudition, foresight and democratic thinking.
3. Our constitution is a reflection of the values, ideals and philosophies embedded in our national consciousness and thought. Through the constitution, citizens and various organisations get their rights and protection.
4. The ideals and principles laid down in the preamble of the constitution determine the basic structure of our constitution. The preamble states that we are committed to making India a sovereign, socialist, secular, democratic republic. It proposes the principles of maintaining justice, freedom, equality and brotherhood in mutual relations towards all citizens.

5. Our constitution established the rule of law and determined the direction to achieve social and economic goals. The intrinsic concepts in the constitution strengthened the structure of social democracy, so that the democracy became stable and strong.
6. The main features of our constitution include Parliamentary Form of Governance, Fundamental Rights, Directive Principles, Secularism, Federalism, Independent Judiciary, Judicial Review, Equality before Law. The constitution adheres to principles of social justice with a strong moral foundation.

   The basic structure of the constitution has evolved over the years and incorporated many of its features gradually, which cannot be tampered with by any government. The distinct feature of our constitution is that it is adapting to the changing times and yet it does not change its original form.
7. While accepting our constitution, those who drafted our constitution chose parliamentary democracy as the system of government for the new republic. This is because in a parliamentary system, the government and its responsibilities are assessed both daily and periodically. It is evaluated daily by the Members of Parliament through discussion on questions, resolutions, no-confidence motions and adjournment motions. Periodic evaluation is done by the voters (public) at the time of election.
8. India is known as the largest and most vibrant democracy in the world. At the heart of our parliamentary system is *janata janardan* (the common man) who has exercised his right to vote 16 times in General Elections through discretion and wisdom. The transfer has been confirmed and the government has changed eight times. Certainly, this is proof of the successful implementation of the

democratic constitution.

9. The interests and aspirations of the neglected class have now gained importance due to the increasing political activism of the masses. The presence of regional and provincial parties has further enhanced the federal character of our politics and helped maintain unity in diversity. The successful completion of the term of the coalition government shows our political maturity.
10. Today we have an independent and active judiciary, a strong system of political parties, a vigilant media system and a vigilant civil society. Our democracy has a number of autonomous bodies, such as the Effective Election Commission, the Central Public Service Commission (UPSC), and the Comptroller and Auditor General (CAG). There is no doubt about the institutional impact of autonomous bodies on governance.
11. The values espoused by any country are recognised by its constitution and it is a matter of pride that when we go abroad, we are respected and honoured everywhere because of India's vibrant democracy, excellent constitution and constitutional order.
12. In the seven decades since our Independence, our Parliament has played a vital role in the progress and development of the nation. Parliament, as the highest democratic institution in the country, is working to embody constitutional values and ideals through legislation to shape a bright future of the society and the country. Through progressive legislation enacted by our Parliament, we have made significant strides in resolving the age-old problems of social discrimination, economic backwardness and political differences.
13. Strong pillars (institutions) have been provided in our constitution as the basic foundation of our democracy. The three most important organs of the state are the

legislature, the administration and the judiciary. They should not work as a competitive centre of government but there should be synergy among all the three pillars. It is the duty of the legislature, the judiciary and the administration to respect each other's jurisdiction, to understand their own limitations and to give each other due respect while discharging their duties within their constitutional framework. This is the best way for the country to make rapid progress.

14. When we adopted this great constitution, there were some hopes and aspirations. Even today, our constitution fulfills the hopes and aspirations of the people and the country. (Perhaps) there may be slight differences between the hopes, aspirations and actual achievements of the time, but in my opinion, the main factors, such as political parties, administration, judiciary and lack of social discipline, are more responsible for it than the constitution.

15. The most significant achievement of the constitution is that we have established the rule of law and considered the principle of equality before law as the very basis.

16. The makers of the constitution made provision of (adult) suffrage (right to vote) for all in the country without any social, economic, political, cultural or religious discrimination and gave equal value to the vote of all. The provision paved the way for social and political empowerment of the deprived sections and fulfilled the expectations and aspirations of the citizens from the constitution.

17. The framers of the constitution put a lot of emphasis on social justice and (positive discrimination) and made provision of special reservation for the weaker sections. As a result, untouchability has almost disappeared from the country. Parliament, the judiciary, social reformers

and religious leaders have made significant contributions to it.

18. Our constitution ensures equal rights and opportunities for all citizens, and for the execution of these rights, there is a system for the general public to go directly to the Supreme Court of the country. The guiding principles of the state enshrined in our constitution are aimed at establishing and protecting a just social order. Our constitution has a unique vision of social harmony and special provision for equality of all religions.

19. The following are some of the important provisions of our constitution which have had a great positive effect on our lives:
    - Article 14 Right to equality
    - Article 15 and 16. Opportunity for reservation to SC, OBC and women
    - Article 19 (a) Freedom of speech and expression. All the citizens have complete right to express their thoughts.
    - Article 19 (c) and Freedom of association or union.
    - Article 19 (d) and Freedom of movement throughout the country.
    - Article 19 (e) and Freedom to practice any profession, occupation, trade, business.
    - Article 21 (Right to life and personal liberty)
    - Includes Protection of life and personal liberty
    - Right to live honourably/respectfully.
    - Right to privacy for all
    - Prisoners in jails or police stations can safely enjoy the same rights as all other citizens.
    - Protection of life
    - Article 21 (a) The right to education is included in the fundamental right.
    - This will save the future of the new generations and

keep them safe.

- Religious freedom is granted to all under Articles 25 to 28.
- Articles 29 and 30 make provisions to protect the rights of religious minorities in the field of culture and education.

20. The above constitutional provision has established our basic philosophy of justice, freedom, equality and fraternal life in the country; it has provided the opportunity for ordinary people to live his life with dignity. This has further strengthened our sense of nationalism – Indianness and belonging.
21. Based on the strength gained from the constitution, Parliament and the government have made significant efforts in the field of women empowerment. As a result, today women in the country are working to their full potential in social, economic and administrative arenas.
22. The country has also made remarkable progress in the fields of agriculture, health and education. Today there are reputed educational institutes, like IIT, IIM which are creating skilled manpower. At the same time, due to the use of new technologies in agriculture, we are now not only self-sufficient but also exporting food grains. Our performance in the medical field is also commendable. Now, medical tourism is also evolving as a business.
23. Despite all this, we cannot be satisfied. We have to fight many challenges along the way. To achieve our goals today, we must work hard in key areas, such as education and literacy, health, nutrition, infrastructure development, farmer welfare and women's safety.
24. I agree that under-representation of women in our legislature is a matter of concern and needs to be addressed.

25. Economic progress has been very fast, but the sense of responsibility and discipline at the previous social level does not seem to have changed at all. Even today, individual interests seem paramount and collective interests are lagging behind. (This is worrisome.)
26. Dr. Rajendra Prasad had conceived the idea of nation-building by following the path of pure character and loyalty. He had said, "Whatever the constitution may or may not provide, the welfare of the country depends upon the way in which the country is administered. That will depend upon the men who administer it. The welfare of the country depends on the manner in which it is run, rather than what the constitution gives or does not give. It depends on the person running the country. If the elected people are capable and men of character and integrity, they would be able to make the best even of a defective constitution, the country better even with a flawed constitution. If they are the only ones (no good at all) the constitution cannot help the country. ["Whatever the constitution may or may not provide, the welfare of the country will depend upon the way in which the country is administered. That will depend upon the men who administer it. If the people who are elected are capable and men of character and integrity, they would be able to make the best even of a defective constitution. If they are lacking in these, the constitution cannot help the country."]
27. Consensus is very important in a democratic system of government. This requires elected representatives to communicate with each other and work together to solve people's problems and build a nation.

I would like to quote one of the many hymns based on the consensus mentioned in the Parliament House:

"Samano mantra: samiti: samani
samanam manah: saha chittamesham.
samannam mantrambhi mantraye vah.
samanen wo havisha juhomi."

(This means that our resolve should be one– we should all make decisions by consensus; our hopes and aspirations should be the same; our consciousness should be full of good feelings; our prayers should be for the welfare of all and our sacrifice should also be for the welfare of all.) Thanks

This particular speech and some other selective speeches by *Taai* were highly praised.

Taai was extremely conscious while speaking. But she was very careful while drafting the write-ups. *Taai's* personal assistant, Pankaj Kshirsagar, shares a wonderful first-hand experience.

"The Lok Sabha session was going on. Taai never left Delhi while the session was on. It was Saturday. We had a very hectic week. On our way home in the evening, *Taai* said, 'There is not much work tomorrow. Just relax.' Of course, we all knew by experience how pointless this talk was!"I received a call from *Taai* around 10 a.m. on Sunday, 'Pankaj, where are you? I made *pohe*, so remembered you.' For us, the people of Indore, getting *pohe* in Delhi, is a feast. I told *Taai* that I was at her residence. Thus, she asked me to come inside to have *pohe*.

"Of course, no matter what day it was or a holiday, at least two of us would be in the office always. We would always keep the office set-up ready! And everyone else would be ready on call. After we had *pohe*, *Taai* said that she wanted to write a letter to the Prime Minister. 'Is a writer, computer operator available?' " 'Everything is ready,' I replied.

"A file of their previous correspondence would be required for reference. I brought it right away. *Taai* sat down to draft a letter. By now, I knew very well who would be useful for the work. So, I told everyone to be ready. One by one, all the office staff joined us.

"*Taai* must have started writing the letter around 11 in the morning but it was completed in the evening. The draft was modified at least eight to nine times. Some word or point or concept needed to be changed! It took a whole day to prepare a 10-line letter! The same was the case with any letter or any speech. If the speech was to be delivered at the international level, then a lot of study was required. If it was in the Lok Sabha, then *Taai* marked the points on the papers. The homework was ready for the anticipated reactions, where and how to speak... so much so, that the speech was almost learnt by heart. And while delivering the actual speech, she would use only a few points if required. We would feel blessed if *Taai* used at least one or two points in her speech out of the several points prepared."

The above speech was also prepared by *Taai* with a lot of efforts. Apart from Lok Sabha, *Taai* had given as many as 190 speeches on important occasions.

□

13

Empowered Women, Empowered Nation

आपणाकरिता शहाणे होती।
ते सहजचि सोये धरिती।
जाणते पणाची महंती।
ऐसी असे॥

Apanakarita shahane hoti.
Te sahajachi soye dhariti.
Janatepanachi mahanti.
Aisi ase.

(Dasbodh, 11.6.17)

(Those who become wise because of the Creator are supportive and loyal to him. Such is the greatness of His wisdom).

—Samarth Ramdas

"Woman is the builder and moulder of a nation's destiny. Though delicate and soft as a lily, she has a heart, far stronger and bolder than of men..." said Rabindranath Tagore.

It is absolutely true in the case of *Taai*. She looks soft and gentle on outside but is tough and strong inside. Her associate Sachin Chaturvedi says, "*Taai* has embodied the three ideals of Rashtra Sevika Samiti– *matrutva* (universal motherhood), *kartrutva* (efficiency and social activism) and *netrutva* (leadership). All the three principles play a pivotal role in her personality. These values are clearly reflected in her thinking, behaviour and decision-making process. She has maintained cordial relations with respected Sindhu Taai Pathak, Hon'ble Pramila Taai Medhe, all the chiefs and other members of the Samiti. She was always inspired by the Samiti's nationalistic ideology and is committed to those values. Even now, she attends the Gurudakshina Utsav in Delhi or Indore, wherever possible."

Suresh Prabhu says, "I was the Chairman of Saraswat Bank. We decided to open a branch of the bank in Indore. The bank was entering Madhya Pradesh for the first time. It was decided to set up a local committee to get acquainted with the new state, language, people, culture and develop new acquaintances and to help solve problems for a smooth business. When we were discussing the names of the members of the committee, naturally Sumitrataai Mahajan's name came up unanimously, but it did not materialise for some reason. She was a MP then. It was then decided to request Sumitratai's husband, Advocate Jayant Mahajan, an upcoming lawyer in Indore. That is how I came in contact with Sumitrataai and her family.

"Her hometown is Konkan and I knew her brother Arun Sathe, who lived in Khar. Soon the professional acquaintance transformed into a cordial family relationship. Various nuances of *Taai's* personalities were unfolded. When I went to meet Shri Mahajan at home for bank work, *Taai* would also be at home.

"*Taai* was a big name, a big leader and a renowned people's representative. I thought she might be proud and conceited, but all the preconception was proved wrong. She was so simple, genial and perfect host. Whenever we went to their house, she personally served us tea and snacks and she never interfered in our conversation."

Taai was proud to be a good housewife. Even today, when she has time, she loves to spend time with her children and grandchildren, prepare their favourite food and appreciate them.

Like most Indian woman, Sumitra Mahajan has always balanced home and work. Every morning before she set out, she would manage all the work in the kitchen. When she entered politics, she had clear views about her priorities. Once she was asked in an interview how she received the support of her husband? *Taai* replied, "When I had a talk with my husband, I promised him that I will do the work only after managing the household responsibilities. I will never behave improperly. And the moment you feel otherwise and tell me to stop, I will leave everything." But luckily that never happened and her husband always supported, appreciated and never interfered in her work.

Her family always remained her first priority. *Taai* may set aside professional work to attend to household chores. *Taai* had said in an interview with journalist Natasha Jha on Danik Bhaskar Channel, "That was one such day when Sushma Swaraj was visiting Indore and I was expected to be part of her entourage." *Taai* was an office bearer of BJP in Madhya Pradesh. Just as she was leaving, her son, who was eight-years old then, asked whether she had made *ladoos* as promised the previous day. She had totally forgotten about it. Her plea that his grandmother would make them for him did not work. He wanted to eat the ones she made. Sumitrataai told Sushma Swaraj to postpone the programme by about an hour. *Taai* made *ladoos* to make her son happy and then continued her work.

Motherhood was the first priority for *Taai*, then came her career while leadership followed. Her priorities were set. She never mixed them up or was never confused about it.

Self-reliance

Taai learnt lessons in self-reliance quite early in life. Her mother died when she was four-years old and she lost her father when she was eleven. Then for further education, she went to her brother in Mumbai and also started working in the Accountant General's office. After her marriage, *Taai* shifted to Indore. She became involved in activities of the Rashtra Sevika Samiti. The procession of 200 women in Indore on the occasion of Rajmata Jijau's death anniversary was a perfect example of her organisational skills. *Taai* was inspired by the character of Lokmata Ahilyabai Holkar and soon her abilities got proper direction. Gradually social and political leadership came her way. She successfully established the identity of a clean and unblemished people's representative and proved her leadership qualities by preserving it for 35 consecutive years (1984 to 2019).

"Women should be involved in politics," Taai feels because "women are not weak". That is what she believed and made it clear from time to time.

She clearly stated this in her first speech abroad after becoming the Speaker of the Lok Sabha.

> *"The worth of any civilisation can be judged from the position it gives to women. Indian culture and ethos justifiably ascribe an honoured status to women. Women are not excluded, but are an integral part of life and dharma. As per the Indian mythology, the concept of woman as 'shakti', or the primal energy force and the concept of 'shiva shakti' or 'ardhnarinateshwar' amply demonstrates that man and woman are not separate entities, but are together and complement each other. They are endowed with similar qualities, capabilities and potential. Woman and man are equal in the eyes of dharma. It is made explicit in a beautiful shloka or verse*

from the Rigveda, which is the oldest Veda and a part of our ancient religious literature. The verse translates somewhat like this:

"'O women! These mantras are given to you equally (as to men). May your thoughts, too, be harmonious. May your assemblies be open to all, without discrimination. Your mind and consciousness should be harmonious. I (the rishi) give you these mantras equally as to men and give you all equal powers to absorb (the full powers) of these mantras.'

"The real need is to change the mindset. The need of the hour is to have self-governance where every individual has the power and every individual is treated equally."

As per the Indian belief, the concept of inclusiveness prevails as men and women are not independent of each other but are interdependent in the family and the larger society.

(From Hon'ble Speaker Sumitra Mahajan's keynote address on the theme 'Building a Conducive Environment for Women's Economic Empowerment' at the ninth annual meeting of women Speakers of Parliament in Geneva, Switzerland, on September 4-5, 2014.)

However, despite this, the representation of women is low at present and special efforts will have to be made to increase it– she expressed the need in her first interview after becoming the Speaker of the Lok Sabha. She said, "Sixty-two women MPs have been elected to the 16th Lok Sabha but I am not satisfied. At least 120 women MPs should be elected. Also, not only numbers but also quality participation is important.

"Compared to men women have more endurance, patience, fortitude, perseverance and ability to perceive people and situations. They also have high physical capacity. Or else, how can a woman do such a difficult job as giving birth to a child? In all other fields, women are working alongside men, but in politics, they are nonchalant or there is apathy. First of all, they should get rid of it. If we want clean politics in India, then more and more women should come forward and join the system."

For this, *Taai* suggested and explained a few steps:

Mindset– From the bottom of their heart, they should decide that politics is their field of work.

Opportunity– The family and society should ensure that a woman gets equal opportunity.

Study– Politics is a different field that requires a lot of study. It requires updated knowledge. If one wishes to speak in the legislature, both research and endurance are required.

Self-reliance– Here no one waits for anyone and no one can depend on anyone.

Struggle– Both men and women have to struggle in life. But women's self-respect is important.

Proving oneself– Nothing remains constant in politics and one has to constantly prove one's worth. It is equally true that women have to prove themselves more vigorously than men because society looks at women from a different perspective.

Restraint– *Aaj nahi to kal* (sooner or later); everyone in politics needs to know it very well because the notions of justice and injustice are unstable here. Conditions are relative.

Dream– Women must chase their dream to enter politics. However, it must be true. It should be real. It should be according to your ability. Its scope should be wider than personal benefits.

Social consciousness– One has to be socially inclined in politics because your existence or non-existence or absence in politics depends on your social consciousness.

Taai cites many examples to explain each point. Many such examples can be noted in this book. When *Taai* joined politics, she had to travel around different areas, including countryside at any time, even at night. *Taai* would never sleep during the journey, no matter how late it was and how tired she was! One of the volunteers was quite curious as he asked, "*Taai*, the journey is so tiring for everybody. Don't you feel sleepy? Don't you feel tired?"

Taai replied, "I do feel drowsy but I don't sleep. I purposely stay awake." *Taai* is always alert and vigilant.

When *Taai* started working in politics, some women, who did not have a political family background but were from RSS families or were involved in various movements, entered into politics and became MPs on their own merits. *Taai's* contemporaries are Sushma Swaraj, Jayavantiben Mehta, Mridula Sinha, Uma Bharti, etc. and many such women today.

Taai received guidance from senior leaders from time to time. After becoming the Speaker of Lok Sabha, *Taai* maintained the same tradition as now she is the senior-most elected MP.

Male MPs often sarcastically remarked that during *Taai's* tenure, if any female MP raised her hand, she was given the chance to speak immediately. Even in the Lok Sabha broadcasts, *Taai* was seen encouraging women MPs. She was above party politics and there were no vested interests. Once Supriya Sule of the Nationalist Congress Party (NCP) stood up to speak and someone from another party started talking very loudly. Supriyataai became a little confused. *Taai* told her from the platform, "Speak, you speak. I have not called their names. He is not given a chance to speak. I have given it to you. So, you continue your talk." Supriyataai continued her speech assertively.

After becoming the Speaker of Lok Sabha, *Taai* tried her best to train the women representatives– MPs and MLAs of the country. Of course, her previous experience was very useful in this work.

Taai was a member of the Joint Committee on the Pre-Natal Diagnostic Techniques (Regulation and Prevention of Misuse) Bill, 1991. She studied the subject thoroughly and worked hard to formulate the Pre-Conception and Pre-Natal Diagnostic Techniques (PCPNDT) Act.

Taai has worked a lot for the development and empowerment of women. She started the Stree Shakti Puraskar to felicitate the common hardworking and diligent women when she was the Women and Child Development Minister. The tradition of the award continues till today. She also started schemes, such as *Swashakti*, *Swadhyay* and *Swadhar*.Earlier, *Taai* was a member and Chairperson of the Women's Empowerment Committee. Each time she thoroughly studied the subjects of the time, submitted reports and recommendations. *Taai* says, "The committee makes recommendations and gives suggestions. It is up to the government to accept it or not. But even if at least 25 to 30% recommendations are accepted, the subject moves further. It generates a kind of pressure on the concerned organisation, the owner or the leader, that they are accountable/answerable to the government. The realisation that there is an authority that can question them can stop a wrongdoing/ injustice."

Addressing a global meeting on the theme 'Building a Conducive Environment for Women's Economic Empowerment' Sumitra Mahajan said that it was their duty to ensure that the laws enacted by legislatures are women-friendly.

She also said that Parliament served as a model institution for creating a positive environment for women's economic empowerment.

"In order to create a more just and caring world, social and economic policies of countries should accord top priority to women empowerment as it is the key to a better life for all."

Taai has often expressed her views on the subject of

women. Right from the earliest days, when International Women's Day was celebrated in 1975, the point that was stressed was 'women's emancipation in society'. It was said that women are helpless, weak and that the society should support them. It was in this context that women were given reservations in *sthanik swarajya sanstha* (local self-government).

When *Taai* was a Member of Parliament, she was a member of the committee for the development of women and children. Her cleverness and maturity of thought was quite evident in her work and in her speeches. Making a strong pitch for women's reservation in Parliament and state legislatures, she said as Lok Sabha Speaker, "It was something that should be given 'respectfully' without any bickering." She was speaking at the valedictory session on the concluding day of the National Women's Parliament in Amaravati.

Addressing a gathering of over 22.000 women, including girl students and delegates from across the globe, Sumitrataai said that empowerment was not women's 'fight with man', but it is to achieve whatever she 'deserved'.

Drawing an analogy between a woman's nature and the course of a river, she said a woman is a brook that does not fight with what comes in its way but diverts and draws a new path. "Like a river, a woman has to make her own path. It is on the banks of a river that life prospers," she added.

Sumitra Mahajan said at the preparatory meeting of the Fourth World Conference of Speakers in New York, "India is fully committed to the promotion of gender equality and utilising information technologies for the empowerment of women. Mainstreaming gender equality is indeed central to the ideal of development. Gender equality and empowerment of women have a critical role to play in the development process, particularly through a multiplier effect."

She added that India was among the early pioneers of

gender empowerment and the country's freedom struggle and subsequent political evolution had given women equal political rights, including at the grassroots level. She said in the context of sustainable development that it was equally important to retain the traditional role of the woman in society, "As the Indian experience ably demonstrates, the woman plays a central role in sustainable development, not only as a mother, but equally importantly as a manager of the household, a unifying factor in the family and as a repository of traditional values which in turn impacts the education and development of the younger generation." She said at the National Conference of Women's Representatives, 2016, that rights, privileges and prestige should not be pleaded; "they are to be earned, accomplished, established, mastered and commanded."

Based on the thoughts of Swami Vivekananda, *Taai* organised a conference on a novel idea – 'How can women representatives in India play an important role in the revival of the nation?'

It was inaugurated on the eve of International Women's Day, 2016, on March 5 and 6 by the President of India, Dr. Pranab Mukherjee. The Speaker of Bangladesh and the president of the Commonwealth Parliamentary Association, Ms. Shirin Sharmeen Chaudhary along with 300 women MLAs, MPs, Union Ministers and Chief Ministers attended the conference. Speaking on the occasion, *Taai* welcomed everyone and also welcomed the announcement by the President earlier to allow women to join the Army and the Air Force.

The uniqueness of the conference was that the women conferences so far were more about revealing how weak women were and demanded equal rights, reservation in elections, etc. But here was a gathering of women who were law makers, ran government and women in power. A convention of resolutions and not demands was the need of the hour. Twenty years had passed since the reservation in local bodies. As a result, women representatives had started to get elected and got their rights. Later, women from Bahujan Samaj (Backward classes) also got the opportunity to get elected at the state level but this was to be done through proper study and preparation. This was the main focus of the conference, which comprised of the main session and the following three supplementary sessions: (i) Contribution to Social Development (ii) Contribution to Economic Development and (iii) Contributing to better Governance and Legislation.

The conference provided women legislators, from across the country, the first-ever platform to interact and learn from their counterparts from all parts of the country and with Union Ministers, Chief Ministers, MPS and eminent women from the judiciary and the bureaucracy.

The interactions and guidance from seniors and experts honed the skills and abilities of the legislators to perform their legislative and non-legislative leadership roles with a sharper and greater effectiveness.

The former President of India, Smt. Pratibha Devisingh Patil also addressed the valedictory session.

The conference equipped the women legislators from across India with latest knowledge in relevant areas and provided them with the right perspective, motivation and guidance in their twin roles – as legislators and as powerful agents of socio-economic progress and change as well of good governance.

It updated them about current national and international issues that are relevant to their field of work as legislators. The proceedings of the conference significantly enhanced their effectiveness, which, in turn, will contribute to nation-building and overall development of a resurgent and inclusive India.

The idea was that women should not only discuss women's

issues but also consider new challenges for the future of the nation. Lok Sabha Speaker Meira Kumar, Chief Minister of Gujarat Anandiben Patel, former Chief Minister of Delhi Sheila Dikshit, Union Minister of External Affairs Sushma Swaraj, Union Minister of Minority Affairs Dr. Najma Heptullah, and Union Minister of Human Resource Development Smriti Irani, Maneka Gandhi, Uma Bharati, Union Minister of Food Processing Industries Harsimarat Kaur Badal, Union Minister of State (Independent Charge) of Commerce and Industry Smt. Nirmala Sitharaman, former Supreme Court judge Smt. Ranjana Desai and former Chief Secretary of Delhi Smt. Shailaja Chandra guided the gathering.

In the evening, famous dancer and MP Hema Malini's dance-drama presentation and Sansad Bhavan Darshan were also included.

The Prime Minister addressed the valedictory session in Central Hall of Parliament House. He stressed on the importance of "women-led development". The Prime Minister said we must think beyond "women's development and move towards women-led development".

Congratulating the Speaker Smt. Sumitra Mahajan for her leadership and vision in the organisation of this conference, the Prime Minister said that in addition to the structured component of such events, experiences shared informally among delegates are also extremely enriching. He added, multi-tasking, which is considered to be a very important element of modern-day management, comes naturally to women.

He also urged the women legislators to engage with their constituents through technology. He described his own experience in this regard and spoke of the enriching thoughts and views he had been receiving through the MyGov platform and Narendra Modi App.

Thanking the Prime Minister and the organising

committee, Taai said, "The time has come for us to gain the position, prestige, strength and equality we need by our capabilities and inner strength, rather than fighting for the provision of reservation for women. And there is no other effective means of advancing this idea than through women MPs."

Though the original idea was by *Taai*, the meeting was organised by young women MPs. Their new ideas made the conference more effective. The meeting was so well received that many similar programmes followed.

The first meeting of BRICS women parliamentarians' forum was held on August 20-21 at Jaipur in Rajasthan. Delegates from Brazil, South Africa, China, Russia and other countries attended the conference. The then Chief Minister of Rajasthan Vasundhara Raje Scindia made sure that all the representatives got a glimpse of the rich Indian culture.

Taai, who was the host, explained the goal of the conference in her speech:

"सर्वस्तरतु दुर्गाणि सर्वे भद्राणि पश्यतु।
सर्व कामनावाप्नोतु सर्व सर्वत्र नन्दतु॥"

(Sarvastratu durgani surve bhadrani pashyatu.
Sarva kamanavapnotu sarva sarvatra nandantu)

It means: "May all cross their difficulties; may all see good and auspicious things. May all get their wishes fulfilled and may everyone everywhere be happy. That is our philosophy. Our goal should be to promote inclusive development and equal responsibility for all people, meaning, all can overcome their problems.

"As women parliamentarians from the BRICS Parliaments, we are here to make a forceful statement that we have a pivotal role in ensuring that all these happen in our respective countries. We must recognise that, as women, we all are concerned with policy issues that affect life at the level of family and community, and other larger social concerns, especially in areas like education, infrastructure and health.

"The role of women parliamentarians as enablers of achievement of the SDGs need to concentrate on our role as people's representatives helping to highlight the concerns of the people as well as mobilizing the participation of the citizens in issues of governance and sustainable development. As women parliamentarians, we also have special responsibilities as well as advantages in providing leadership to women and grassroots organisations, which are engaged in addressing issues like climate change.

"We, as parliamentarians, have various roles – legislative, representational and leadership. As legislators, we can bring our knowledge and understanding of topical issues and also concerns about the SDGs and their implementation to bear on the content of legislative proposals. Our representational roles extend to our engagement with the governance processes to represent the concerns of our constituencies helping the government define development priorities and supporting them in their implementation. Parliamentarians also have the leadership roles in that. In that, we can provide leadership too and mentor elected representatives at the grassroots – that is more important—and help initiate development projects and local bodies in securing funding for their own projects."

She also referred to her efforts to 'save daughter, teach daughter'.

She concluded by quoting a Sanskrit prayer,

"जीवनेयावद आदानं श्यात प्रदानं ततोधिकम,
इत्येशाप्रार्थना अस्माकम् भगवन परिपूर्यतम्।"

Indian philosophy believes in the commitment of returning back more than what one receives. In the prayer, we say, "Oh God, please keep my mental framework such that I always remain committed for giving more than receiving."

Speaking on the topic 'Innovative Practices for the Care of Elderly Women in India" on 5 August, 2016, she commented on the current plight of elderly women. She referred to Mark Twain's famous statement 'Age is a state of mind, if you don't mind; it does not matter' and that old age is a gift to live happily and mentally. She also advised everyone to make their lives meaningful by doing so.

"Women are the fountainhead of life, the family, the society, the community and the country. Go around the women and it is she who holds the world together. Women are the natural care-givers. They are the first providers, the first educators, the first resource allocators in the family and society, and they are the protectors of the environment. In households, women are often the primary energy managers and are more likely than men to conserve energy through a greater willingness to alter everyday behaviours."

Taai, as a staunch supporter of women's power, insists that she should get what she deserves. Whenever *Taai* got the opportunity, she stressed her thoughts vigorously.

The significance of the national conference of women legislators, New Delhi in 2016 was appreciated by NITI Ayog. The two-day national conference on the theme 'We for Development' was organised at the initiative of the Lok Sabha Speaker Sumitra Mahajan on March 10-11, 2018. The conference, hosted under the auspices of the Indian Parliamentary Group, was inaugurated by Prime Minister Narendra Modi and was attended in large numbers by MPs, MLCs and MLAs from across the country.

An exhibition on 'We for Development' will be displayed by the Parliamentary Museum and Archives, Lok Sabha Secretariat.

Amitabh Kant, CEO, NITI Aayog made a presentation on the working of aspirational districts and how the women legislators can contribute to it. The conference comprised a plenary session on the theme 'We for Development' and two working sessions on 'Role of Legislators in Development

Process' and 'Optimum Utilisation of Resources in Development'. The resolution by Om Birla was accepted by all the delegates. Union Road Transport and Highways Minister Nitin Gadkari addressed the valedictory session of the conference and *Taai* thanked the participants and inspired all women legislators and gave them confidence that they can contribute to nation building.

Earlier women's conferences were held specifically to advance the demands of women. But according to *Taai*, a woman who is basically capable, can do a lot for the nation. The conferences organised on the occasion of International Women's Day guided the empowered women public representatives about how they could play a proactive role in the development of the country.

With her efficient leadership, *Taai* gave the right direction to women power with the *mantra* of 'do not ask, contribute'.

□

Empowered women Empowered Nation –Song Ummidam	
https://youtu.be/hvdssbiJ5hY	

Hon'ble Sumitrataai Mahajan's speech in Women's Conference	
https://www.youtube.com/watch?v=DPu45RMwCz0	

14
Traveling on Mission

देखोन ऐकोन जाणती।
शहाणे अंतर परिक्षिती।
धूर्त ते अनवघेंच समजती।
गुप्तरूपे॥

Dekhona Aikona janati.
Shahane antara parikshiti.
Dhurta te anavaghecha samajati.
Guptarupe.

(Dasbodh, 15.7.29)

(The wise look, listen and understand by examining the mind. They inwardly understand everything quietly and secretly.)

—Samarth Ramdas

It is true that travels make man more competent and efficient. After becoming the speaker of Lok Sabha, yet another responsibility came her way. She had to show and represent the image of Indian parliament abroad. For that she had to travel extensively and prepared herself accordingly.

She had to travel within the country and abroad. Taai visited capitals of almost all states, the main purpose of the visits was to make common people aware of Lok Sabha and have qualitative dialogue with the elected representatives in the legislative assembly and the legislative council.

Her visits were, of course, pre-planned. The concerned people were already informed. Her visit was an official visit as a constitutional office bearer. She made it a point to meet eminent personalities, medical professionals, engineers, business, social and political leaders in the area. She tried to talk to them about their problems, and ensure a brief overview of local and national developments. She preferred to hold separate meetings with women. She encouraged them to come forward in politics, advised women MLAs to learn new things and to get involved in extensive studies.

She took great interest in ancient temples and made it a point to visit ancient temples, meet saints and leading spiritual gurus there and take blessings from them.

She also enjoyed talking to local journalists. Press conferences were often organised. Sumitratai always believed in thorough studies, so she was well-prepared for the press conferences. Thus the press conferences were always stimulating and fascinating.

Taai insisted on treating her colleagues or the Secretariat staff equally.

Taai holds special memories of meeting with Najma Heptullah in Northeast India. In addition, she transplanted an old tree in Shillong.

Meeting Lata Mangeshkar on 28 September, 2018 was another memorable incident.

Lataji's sister Meena Khadikar wrote a book on Lata Mangeshkar titled, 'Mothi tichi Savli'. The book was released by Lok Sabha Speaker Sumitra Mahajan on September 28 at Ravindra Natya Mandir in Mumbai. Shivshahir Babasaheb Purandare was also present on the occasion. Vidyavachaspati Pt. Shankar Abhyankar addressed the gathering. 'Anandghan', a program of popular songs composed by Latadidi was presented by 'Hridayesh Arts' in association with 'Swargandhar'. Pt. Hridaynath Mangeshkar anchored the programme while songs were performed by Usha Mangeshkar, Vibhavari Apte, Madhura Datar, Sonali Karnik, Prajakta Satardekar.

Many foreign delegations visit India. In the past, most of the international meetings were held in Delhi. Due to Taai's initiative, some international conferences were organised in different prominent places in India. Taai organised many international conferences at various places in India to give a glimpse of India's cultural richness to international visitors.

She travelled extensively all over the country. The Indian Parliamentary Group (IPU) was established in 1949 and serves as the main branch of the Inter-Parliamentary Union and the Commonwealth Parliamentary Organization. It consists mainly of the Speaker of the Legislative Assembly and the Legislative Council of India. They have regular meetings where ideas are exchanged, problems are discussed and suggestions are offered. As the Speaker of the Lok Sabha, Taai was the ex-officio President of the Federation (Union) and was in touch with the Legislative Assembly Speakers of all the States. Taai had some great interactions not only in the states where the Bharatiya Janata Party was in power but also in other states. Taai specifically mentions Bihar Assembly Speaker Shri Vijay Chaudhary who was very simple, gentle, knowledgeable and studious. When the meeting of the IPU was held in Bihar, Shri Vijay Chowdhury welcomed everyone warmly and made excellent arrangements.

Taai also makes special mention of the conference in Uttar Pradesh where Shri. Akhileshji Yadav's Samajwadi Party was in power. All the arrangements of the council were meticulous and well- handled and the conference in Uttar Pradesh was useful.

Such conferences provided an opportunity for Taai to get along with all kind of people. She always tried to interact not just with people's representatives but also with the volunteers, businessmen, professionals and women's groups. Thus, she always remained connected with the masses.

She also stressed the point in the meetings with the distinguished representatives of society. Taai met some activists and women representatives at the Women's Science Conference in Bangalore. Some vegetable sellers from different villages attended the meet. While sharing their problems the women said, "When they bring vegetables from their village in bus, the heavy baskets with vegetables have to be loaded on top. We don't want to ask help from men because they often misbehave on pretext of help, our problem could be solved if some compartments are made inside the bus near the windows to keep the baskets, we would also become self-sufficient." Another women's group mentioned that the tools to work in farms were quite heavy and big for women and expressed the need to modify the tools as per the needs and problems of women.

In her speech Taai expressed that the scientific research should aim at lessening the miseries of common people, "Women scientists should strive to modify the research and improve the technology as per the needs and make women-friendly tools that can be easily used by them."

Taai always asked the Speakers of the Legislative Assemblies and the people's representatives, to be concerned about the national interest. We should work for the national cause. The dignity, the role and the position we hold is beyond any party. We need to use the position in the interest of the nation.

Taai's colleague Shri. Rama Duttaji hints at Taai's love for shopping. "She loved to shop, but she was very particular about the payments and keeping accounts. She herself paid for all the purchases made. I handled all her cash. After the purchase, she would look back to ensure that I paid for the purchases. Otherwise the local activists would offer to pay, she never allowed that. Also, all the gifts received during the visit were duly listed and given to the Lok Sabha Museum. The receipt of submission of the list needed to be given to Taai. And she checked it without fail.

Lok Sabha Speaker Sumitra Mahajan led many parliamentary delegations abroad.

Taai mentioned some of the memorable incidents in details.

Honorary Doctorate "D. Lit." from South Korea

In South Korea, Taai was awarded an honorary doctorate ('D .Lit.').

Hankuk University of Foreign Affairs (HUFS) conferred Honorary Doctorate on Lok Sabha Speaker Smt. Sumitra Mahajan, in Seoul on 30 September, 2016.

In her Acceptance speech, Smt. Mahajan said, "I am honoured to receive an honorary doctorate from the prestigious HUFS University. The honour assumes special significance as the public rarely recognizes the work of Parliamentarians. There is a strong commonality between the work that is done at a University, and at the legislature of any democracy, as they both are at the service of the people. HUFS's honourary doctorate is a symbol of the commonalities that bind the two professions, and their objectives, both as academics and as legislators. This honour is recognition of both as in her personal capacity and as an elected representative of Indian people. I accept the Honorary Doctorate in that spirit, and in the recognition of HUFS's support for shared objectives of improving mutual understanding.

According to Samyug Yusa (The Heritage History of the Three Kingdoms), Suriratna, the princess of Ayodhya, reached the Busan region of South Korea by sea in the 13th century. She married a local prince and a few years later he became King Kim Suro. She came to be known as Queen Heo Hwang-ok. They were very popular rulers. It is said that a lot of people of Indian descent from Ayodhya live in South Korea. Out of a total population of 5 crores, 50 lakh people are of mixed race. They still consider themselves to be of Indian descent. The princess carried many valuable things, such as gold, coins, and jewels along with her. There were large boats in the past and large quantities of stones and boulders of the same weight were kept in it in order to maintain the balance. A memorial and stones at that time still exist in South Korea. The legend of Queen Heo is inscribed on the stone memorial in Korean and English. When Taai visited the memorial she realised that the local people regard even a small piece of stone at the place extremely auspicious and the government preserves it as a precious cultural treasure. In a way stones of Ayodhya are worshipped and preserved in South Korea. Taai was quite pleased to know the legend signifying the cultural exchange between India and South Korea. Since a large number of Koreans trace their ancestry to Heo Hwang-ok, hundreds of South Korean tourists visit Ayodhya every year to pay tributes to their Queen. Hon'ble Prime Minister Shri Narendra Modiji has reserved a place for Queen Hoe's memorial near Ayodhya and it is a historical symbol of friendship between India and South Korea.

In South Korea, there is an interesting custom of spreading a sheet at a time of funeral. Everyone who comes to console the diseased family offers some amount as donation according to his own ability. This provides immediate support to the family of the deceased.

Also, at the time of marriage ceremony, two boxes for bride and groom are kept at the place and guests fill the boxes with gifts and money. The amount is then collected and divided between the bride and groom's family as needed.

These practices are observed in a very simple and wholesome manner. Even in our culture, there are traditions and customs that express harmony and cooperation.

Taai also highlights the exemplary progress by South Korea in a span of 25 years. Now we see a multi-storied bridge being built one on top of the other. South Korea has built it long ago. The administration, the rulers and the people are all motivated to work for the progress of the nation. The country is overwhelmed with patriotism.

Mongolia-India Link

Taai's visit to Mongolia was also a memorable one. Mongolia is a landlocked country in East Asia bordered by China and Russia. We consider Genghis Khan, as a cruel attacker. But in Mongolia, Genghis Khan is the 'Father of the Nation'. Taai could know this story during her visit to Mangolia. His statue is erected in front of Parliament. They consider him emperor. Genghis Khan's Mongol Empire covered much of Central Asia and China. He did not lose a single battle. Due to his military success, Genghis Khan is considered to be the first emperor. He brought the Silk Road into a single system of government. This facilitated communication and trade between Northeast Asia, Muslim Southwest Asia, and Christian Europe, expanding cultural horizons.

Mongolia is a desert region. It takes a lot of hard work to live here and for that he had to loot food or money from another place. The closest non-desert region to it was China, Iran, Iraq and Afghanistan at that time, which were relatively dense and rich, so there were a lot of battles between them.

Genghis Khan was a valiant warrior. He used to make raids and loot wealth from there and feed his people. Therefore, Genghis Khan is considered a hero in Mongolia. After returning to his kingdom, he would stay in jungles for three to four months, giving away all his gold, coins and possessions. He knew that what he had done was bad, and the people believed that he went to remote areas as a punishment for his misdeeds.

799 years ago, in 1221, the great Mongol conqueror Genghis Khan of the Indus River Arrived on the west coast near the town of Kalabagh in Punjab with 50,000 troops. He conquered Iran, Turkmenistan, Uzbekistan, parts of Kazakhstan, Tajikistan, Kyrgyzstan and present-day Afghanistan, much of what was then north-western India. He destroyed the great cities of Samarkand, Bukhara, Nishapur, Otrar and Gurganj. He destroyed the Islamic Centre. His forces burned Islamic libraries and replaced mosques with Buddhist temples. He exempted Buddhist monasteries from taxation because they served his empire, but banned Islamic practices, such as halal. He considered Muslims and Jews as 'slaves'. Genghis Khan respected women and constantly consulted his mother and wives. But there are rumours that he did not invade India. There is also an opinion that Genghis Khan refused to invade India for religious reasons, as Hindustan is the birthplace of Hinduism and Buddhism. The ancient polytheistic belief system in Mongolia, called Tangrizism in English, is very similar to Hinduism. Buddhism has existed in Mongolia for almost two thousand years. Kublai Khan, the grandson of Genghis Khan, adopted Buddhism as the state religion of the Mongol Empire. Today most Mongolians are Buddhists and they follow Tibetan Buddhism.

Indian Parliamentary Delegation led by Lok Sabha Speaker Smt. Sumitra Mahajan visited Gandategchinlen Monastery. Gandategchinlen Monastery is a Tibetan-style Buddhist monastery in Mongolian capital, Ulan Bator. The name stands for 'Great Place of Complete Joy', and the monastery is a house of 150 monks. Featuring a 26.5 metres high statue of *Avalokitesvara,* the monastery came under the State protection in 1994. 13th Dalai Lama went to stay there in 1904, he is still worshipped there. The tall Avalokitesvara temple was built in 1913. In 1925, the temple for keeping the remains of the 8th Jebtsundamba Khutuktu was built. It is now the monastery library. Since 1992, the Supreme Leader of the Centre of All Mongolian Buddhists and Abbot of Gandantegchinlen Monastery has been Lama Gabju Choijamts Demberel.

After Gandategchinlen Monastery, the Members of Indian Delegation also visited Pethub Monastery. Besides, interacting with the monks of the Monastery, Smt. Mahajan also visited a photo exhibition on the life and times of 19th Kushok Bakula Rinpoche. She observed that the Pethub Monastery is an enduring symbol of Indo-Mongolian spiritual relationship.

Sumitra Mahajan led a delegation consisting of Members of Parliament from both Lok Sabha and Rajya Sabha to Moscow and had an honour to address Russian Parliament.

Extracts from speech of Hon'ble Speaker of Lok Sabha Smt. Sumitra Mahajan in The State Duma on 12 July, 2017

India and Russia share age-old relations. In the 15th Century, Russian traveller Afanasy Nikitin visited India and shared his memories with Russian people through his book 'Journey Beyond the Three Seas'. This is the first written source which brought Indian culture closer to the Russian people. I am proud to state that Leo Tolstoy and Mahatma Gandhi were two luminaries of the same mindset. Tolstoy's book 'The Kingdom of God is Within You' influenced Mahatma Gandhi in a significant manner.

This year we are celebrating the 70th anniversary of the establishment of diplomatic relations between India and Russia in a grand manner. More than 150 events are being held in both countries in this regard. We are also organising the 'Namaste Russia' programme in Russia.

I would like to thank our Russian friends for the successful organization of the 3rd International Day of Yoga in 68 regions of Russia.

Speaking in the assembly at Saint Petersburg, on the subject of 'Promoting cultural pluralism and peace through Inter-faith and inter-ethnic dialogue', Sumitra Mahajan explained many aspects of cultural diversity. Indian society is based on spiritualism, humanism and gives less importance to materialistic growth. She stressed that India is socially, politically, culturally, religiously and spiritually democratic. As a result, a number of religions and religious ideas have taken birth and flourished in India. India is one of the largest and most plural societies in the world. Pluralism is not diversity alone, but energetic engagement with diversity. Various languages, music, dance and art forms have developed in India. India's accommodating ethos has sheltered many religions coming from outside her boundaries and its spread has never been oppressive in character; rather it is educative and elevating. Wherever Indians travelled they not only left their foot marks but left spiritual and cultural impressions on the hearts of people. We have shown to the world that different religions, languages, traditions, customs and faiths can have peaceful co-existence. A nation's culture resides in the hearts and the soul of its people. India believes in the culture of giving and donating:

गौरवं प्राप्यते दानात् न तु वित्तस्य संचयात्।
स्थितिः उच्चैः पयोदानां पयोधीनां अधः स्थितिः ॥

Dignity/fame is obtained by donating, not by accumulating wealth. The clouds that give away water stand high, whereas the sea that just gathers it stays low.

Taai often quoted appropriate Sanskrit verses in her speeches that added profoundness to the speech.

Paradise in the Desert

When Taai visited Dubai, she was amazed at its splendour. She was impressed how one of the driest regions on earth has been transformed into a beautiful city with gardens and fountains. She thought, "Oh, if man can do so much in desert, then why can't we do it here?" she pondered over this thought many times. Dubai has a large Indian population. They are now allowed to build different types of temples there.

"Why can't we make such progress in today's world where professionalism is the only religion?" This question, however, always haunted her mind.

There are many temples of Buddha in Japan. Sumitratai feels that Japan is spiritually connected to India. Taai was received with love and respect even in Japan.

Sita's Foreign Policy

Taai was particularly keen to visit Ashoka Vatika and other famous places referred to in the Ramayana, when she visited Sri Lanka. Sita was kept as captive by the Demon King Ravana after her abduction from Dandakaranya. How frightening it would be to live in the garden surrounded by dense forest and mountains? How could she face the situation in the unknown area with no means of communication? However, Sitaji made friendship with the locals in the area. According to Ramayana, a demon named Trijata used to guard her. Sita and Trijata shared a great bond of love and friendship. When Ravana took away Sita through the sky, and misled her by telling that Lakshmana and all the army were dead and was trying to persuade her to accept him, it was Trijata who helped Sita.

Taai considers it an example of a good foreign policy. No matter how serious the problem may be, the solution could be worked out. 'This is taught in our mythological texts. We need to think positively about that.' she feels.

Experiences in other Countries

Taai could find joy in even small things in life. Perhaps that's what she cherished most.

While Taai was on her visit to South Africa, local officials took the delegation on a jungle safari. Everyone noticed that two giraffes were walking along the road. Taai had the chance to see a catwalk of giraffes in the woods. Taai notes, "I was very happy to see the scene and enjoy the chemistry between the two animals. For the first time in my life, I realised that a giraffe is a very beautiful, handsome and graceful animal.

Once she ordered some local vegetarian food in the state of South America. She found the Mexican food quite close to Indian food. Many times she realised that many foods in the world are quite similar to the food in India.

She also had great experiences in South Asian countries and Indonesia. Taai travelled at many places but every time she had the same desire to learn, acquire new experiences. Though she was on official tours and had to attend conferences and meetings as the Speaker of Lok Sabha, she never lost chance to learn some new aspect of the local culture, religion, tradition, history and general life style of the country. She always compared them with India and many times found similarities between the cultures.

She had an official invitation to give speech on every foreign tour. These scholarly speeches were patriotic, contained Sanskrit proverbs, mentions of great personalities like Goddess Ahilyabai, meaningful references to cultural heritage, references to India's mythological, historical and spiritual ties with other countries. She equally respected cultures and traditions of the country where she visited.

She constantly gave thought to implementing good things from abroad in India. Taai took a lot of interest in finding commonalities and cultural, historical links between India and other countries. Mauritius shares manifold similarity with India. The ancestors of today's citizens in Mauritius were taken there from India as labourers. Mauritius still has temples of Lord Shiva and Lord Vishnu. Ganga Talao Lake in Mauritius is a very popular pilgrim place that has gained popularity, When Taai visited Mauritius she had carried Gangajal from Haridwar with her and faithfully offered it to Ganga Lake.

Taai realised during her visits abroad that India holds a place of reverence among people of the world. It is because we never went there with the intention of occupying any part. We tried to establish amiable ties with different countries and spread the message of universal brotherhood and compassion. Taai aimed to spread the same message of ***'Vasudhaiva Kutumbakam'*** all over the world!

□

Hon'ble Sumitrataai Mahajan addressing Russian Parliament	
https://www.youtube.com/watch?v=KbDB1bwxhdU	

15
Virtuous and Versatile

लोक पारखून सांगावे।
राजकारणे अभिमान झाडावे।
पुन्हा मेळवून घ्यावे।
दुरील दोरे॥

Loka parakhuna sangave.
Rajakarane abhimana zadave.
Punha melavuni ghyave.
Durila dore.

(Dasbodh, 11.5.20)

(Examine people well to find who to keep away from and astutely remove pride from others diplomatically and work to bring people together who have become distant from each other).

—Samarth Ramdas

Indore and *Taai* are inseparable. They hold an intimate bond. Indore stands testimony to *Taai's* growth as a political leader and *Taai* strove for the development of her workplace like a mother. She has imprinted an invincible mark on Indore.

Sumitratai was elected a people's representative from Indore in 1984 and she represented Indore in the Lok Sabha for 30 consecutive years, since 1989. She says in a lighter tone, "Journalists often asked me questions regarding Indore. I asked them, 'You have elected me as an MP, then why don't you ask me about the issues at national level? There are other people's representatives for Indore. They are doing good work. Why don't you ask them on local issues?' But the journalist maintained, 'We have neither been to Delhi nor have chance to see Lok Sabha? Indore is our world'." *Taai* says, "This was something I always remembered. Your roots, your foundation should be firm and fixed" and that is the secret of her continual victory!

Taai took part in the politics of Madhya Pradesh and worked on women's fronts across the country. She led effectively at the national level and handled various subjects at the Centre; yet, she remained rooted to her base – the RSS ideology and Indore. She may reside in Indore or Delhi but she always remains connected. Her existence was always felt in Indore. People never felt disappointed and the work was not hampered just because *Taai* was out of town. Well-organised office, competent staff, closely connected people from varied localities of the city, strong and intimate force of dedicated volunteers and workers– were *Taai's* biggest strength.

Taai can be called 'Indore's subjective Google Map!' She accurately knew the addresses of her associates and had a perfect know-how about various development works in different localities. Whether she was in Indore or not, her office remained open all 365 days a year from 10.30 a.m. to 7.30 p.m. Furthermore, office assistants were available as per need. Moreover, everyone was assured that *Taai* would help whenever required.

The urbanisation was inevitable over time. The population of Indore increased from 9 lakhs to 30 lakhs. She was instrumental in bringing the basic and state-of-the-art facilities required for this. This was because she

was well-organised in her work. Her vision had clarity–

one person, one responsibility– each person well aware of the concerned subject. She concentrated on eight pillars of development:

1. Railways– buses (public transport)
2. Roads– sewers
3. Civil aviation
4. Water– electricity
5. Toilets– crematorium– hygiene
6. Empowerment of women
7. Sports and cultural activities
8. Development works

Taai ran a very hectic schedule in Delhi and handled various challenges, forever alert and taking keen interest in development work at Indore. The scope of work varied– developing infrastructure, health care facilities, well-equipped hospitals, etc. She would never leave Delhi when the Parliament was in session; otherwise, she would fly to Indore on Friday evening and stay there till Monday morning. The moment she boarded the plane, she would start the work regarding Indore. Meetings with concerned individuals, government officials and associates were planned in the plane itself. She would go to the place of work directly from the airport. Meetings, inauguration functions, supervision work, social visits, etc. the list continued till she boarded the flight to Delhi on Monday.

On other days of the week also *Taai* maintained contact with Indore from Delhi. She reviewed the work in the Indore office regularly every evening and planned the work schedule for the next day. Tated sir often accompanied her. If the need arose, Tated sir would look into the matter immediately. *Taai* would personally contact the concerned officials to find the solution. She was more concerned with the completion of work than about pride, position or honour.

Advocate Nagesh Namjoshi handled the responsibility of railway work. In fact, he was a disciple of *Taai's* husband, advocate Jayant Mahajan. When *Taai* got involved in social and then political work, on the advice of Jayantrao, Nagesh started helping *Taai* and the association continues till date! Nagesh knew his subject well. He did all research work, homework, verification of all documents, information of concerned officers, expected problems in tackling the subject and carrying out follow-up every five days.

He says, "Between 2014 and 2019, three new trains were started from Indore and three trains were extended. Except for the northeast and Jharkhand, direct connectivity was started with all the state capitals in the country. It was perhaps for the first time that the record of starting eight new trains in a year was established. Permission for the construction of new railway lines, approval and implementation of a proposal costing around 3,000-3,500 crore rupees for the ongoing construction and permission for electrification and building a double track were some of the achievements. The widening of the Fatehabad-Ujjain route (earlier the railway authorities were not willing) was approved. It benefited the people of Indore to a great extent.

One of the five oldest railway lines in the country and an important railway line in terms of tourism, which was started by Holkar Maharaj in 1877, was known as Holkar State Railway. The Railway Ministry decided to preserve the beautiful Mhow-Patalpani route, which was 140-years old, as a permanent 'Heritage Trek'. Approval was taken to renew it.

The gradient of the slope was changed from 1:40 to 1:150 (gradient refers to the change rate of a slope. Take for instance, a gradient of slope that is 1 in 40 (1:40). A 1:40 slope means that for every 40 metres along the ground, the slope height increases by 1 metre.) The project to run the heritage train with vistadome coaches was successful because of *Taai*. Now the route has become very popular.Nagesh Namjoshi shares a heartfelt incident. Once he went to the Railway Ministry in Delhi for some work. Sadananda Gowda was the Railway Minister then. The work was simple, but was not getting done. After the follow-up, when he reached Taai's residence at 8th Gurudwara, Rakabganj Marg, that was 10 minutes away from the Railway Bhawan, he received a phone call that the work was done.

Nagesh Namjoshi informs, "Development work sometimes required acquisition of land; but *Taai* insisted that if the field was sown before the displacement, it should not be occupied until the harvest and if there was a house, an alternative location should be sought."Sumitratai followed certain rules while implementing new projects. She never got involved in transfers, contracts and appointments, nor did she interfere in these matters.

There was no direct train from Indore to Konkan and despite all efforts, the railway authorities were not ready. When Suresh Prabhu was the Railway Minister, while discussing in the Railway Board, someone mentioned that *Taai's* native place was Konkan and people there were demanding a direct train to Indore, Suresh Prabhu, who too came from the same area, saw to it that the train was started.Suresh Prabhu shares some fond memories of *Taai* when he say, "We presented the railway budget. I was quite stressed as I had to present the budget for the first time. *Taai* supported me, encouraged me and helped me. When I presented the budget second time, *Taai* asked me on a lighter note, 'Is the train on the right tracks now?' *Taai* was quite persistent and keen on the Indore-Manmad railway line. When the Indore-Manmad railway line was sanctioned , *Taai* held a meeting with the MPs (from constituencies on the line) to express gratitude on behalf of all. In fact, she was the president; it was a very high position. I was impressed by her expression of gratitude. I was quite fascinated by her attitude and style of working," Whether *Taai* was in Indore or not, her office was open to the public. This responsibility was efficiently managed by office-incharge Yogesh Vartak. He adhered to *Taai's* principles of honesty and integrity. Accurate accounts were maintained by the office. The image of a leader depends largely on the people working in his or her office. *Taai* is blessed with a strong group of dedicated and honest office associates.

Although the number of visits to Indore decreased when she became the Speaker of the Lok Sabha, her focus on the development of Indore did not diminish. Rajesh Mishra often accompanied her on Delhi-Indore trips. By experience, he could very well understand *Taai's* requirements and thoughts. Krishna Upadhyay communicated her programmes and thoughts through the social media.

Before becoming Speaker, *Taai* focused on providing the basic services. Roads have now been built in every village, but she insisted on building gutters for sewage disposal too. Roads should be built in rural areas; 20,000-km roads and bridges were built over them. The means of transport connected 500 villages out of 658 villages. *Taai* studied the schemes, such as the Pradhan Mantri Gram Sadak Yojana and the Central Road Fund, and paid attention that the constituency derived its benefits.

Road widening was a major issue in terms of development.

Minister of Public Works Nitin Gadkariji was making a statement on the Delhi-Mumbai Express Highway in the Lok Sabha. It was not directly linked with Indore then. *Taai* reminded that if Ujjain, Garot and Indore road could be connected in Mandsaur district, it would be beneficial for Indore. Nitin Gadkariji immediately gave approval to the six-lane widening of Garot-Indore road. Many development projects were carried out, including a four-lane state highway, beautification of the cities, etc.

The National Automotive Test Tracks (NATRAX) is a unique project located at Pithampur in Dhar district. The 11.3-km auto-testing track has been developed on more than 3,000 acres of land. Vehicles can be driven at a speed of 300 kms per hour and 14 automobile testing tracks are constructed. It is Asia's longest and the world's fifth high-speed test track. Vehicles come here for capacity testing from various places in India.

Taai made significant contributions in the field of sports, arts and culture. Mukund Dravid and Vasant Masker, *Taai's* dedicated associates in the field, worked hard to make Indore a sports hub. She constructed a stadium and also started a residential academy. More than 300 players received scholarships and sports equipment each year besides receiving the required training in the field. She consciously encouraged Indian games, such as Kho-Kho, Kabaddi and worked hard to develop a sports culture in the area. National Kho-Kho Championships for women were also held.

A branch of Sports Authority of India (SAI) was established. A sports complex was built on 11 acres of land with a fund of Rs. 4 crores. She focused on its professional use to encourage arts, sports, drama and dance.

Till now three players from Indore have received the Arjuna Award. Juhi Jha, the girl living in Sulabh Shauchalay won the state level Vikram Puraskar in Kho-Kho. Some have even received the Dronacharya Award. She did not allow any encroachment on any ground.

Taai's contribution in a variety of fields is praiseworthy indeed, but the role of her dedicated team of associates is no less important. Devraj Singh Parihar helped her in rural development. Rural areas faced water scarcity in summers. The tanker had to be used to supply water. For this, tankers were given to many *gram panchayats*. This made it easier to fetch water. Two or three years later, a representative of the company visited the place to check all the tankers and offered to do repair work and maintenance free of cost. All the transactions with the company were so transparent that he felt it was his 'moral responsibility' and he fulfilled it. Every human being is good and upright; *Taai* invoked goodness in every one.

Roads, water, electricity are the three foundations of good governance in villages. *Taai* added the fourth one to it – village crematorium! Earlier, in rural areas, it was customary to set dead bodies on fire in an open space. *Taai* made arrangements to erect four iron pillars and a platform for cremation in various villages. She convinced the people to build crematoriums with the help of public donations. Making use of MP funds, she built over three lakh shades and many crematoriums. Earlier 500 kg of wood was required for burning dead bodies; now it came down to 150 kg, saving both labour and trees and reduced pollution. An honest worker looking after MP funds handled this social responsibility for 30 long years. *Taai* could select and assign appropriate work to suitable people and they carried out the responsibilities like a mission. She could skillfully connect with the right people and retained them to fulfill the social cause.

Taai had been an MP eight times – this is a short sentence. However, why and how it was achieved is an extensive case study – incessant dedicated strivings for over 25 years.

Her personal assistant Vandana Mhaskar points out, "Working with Hon'ble Sumitrataai has taught me a lot about how to talk, how to answer, how to prioritise work. I have also learnt how to be firm and not accept anything if someone tried to offer/ pay for the work done and be extra careful while doing the work next time.

Secondly, since 1998, we have been sending condolence letters to the mourning families of the deceased in Indore on a daily basis. The list included people of acquaintances, leaders of all parties, activists, relatives and friends. I used to send SMS giving the required phone numbers, the background information about the departed soul and without fail *Taai* contacted the mourning families from wherever she was. Her assuring words not only provided solace to the families but also earned respect for her. Later *Taai* visited the family when she came to Indore. Her programme was communicated to *mandal pramukhs*, head of women's wing and prominent workers in the area in advance so that they could accompany *Taai*.

"*Taai* also calls the volunteers and associates on their birthdays. Every day, I send her SMS detailing the names and phone numbers of those celebrating their birthday on the day. Many volunteers eagerly wait for her calls.

"If any artist from Indore received a special award, a student excelled or a photographer received an award, *Taai* would promptly appreciate the achievement by making a phone call. She even wishes leaders and volunteers of different faiths on their festivals. People also call and greet her on all important days...

No matter how busy *Taai* is, she replies to all the messages. If she is invited for a programme outside the region, then she would consult the concerned authorities and volunteers in the area, take the necessary information and then agree or disagree to attend the programme. She always remained connected with the local volunteers. Many a times she would prefer to dine at a volunteer's home than in a hotel. She never allowed any special arrangements for her and enjoyed sharing food with the volunteers.

Taai receives many applications regarding financial help for studies/waiving off fees. Many eminent personalities offer to help. The help is provided only after through scrutiny of the needy students. Proper records are kept. Students are made aware that "someone has made arrangement for your fee today. When you complete your studies and start earning, then you should be prepared to help the needy students. The cycle of help should continue."

This book is not a portrayal of an individual named Sumitra Mahajan. It is not an attempt to glorify her or critical analysis of her work; it is an attempt to give an insight into the journey of a people's representative, a versatile and competent woman who was elected from the constituency for 30 consecutive years. It lists many contributions of a clean, tough, a battle-hardened political leader who rose from the ranks to the top post of Lok Sabha Speaker.

□

16

Padma Bhushan Beacon of Light

पाहतां तरी सांपडेना।
किर्ती करू तरी राहेना।
आले वैभव अभिळासीना।
काही केल्या॥

Pahata tari sapadena.
Kirti karu tari rahena.
Ale vaibhava abhilasina.
Kahi kelya.

(Dasbodh, 11.5.24)

(It is difficult to find a genuine person in politics even after searching high and low. But when people want to praise a genuine person, he is not enamoured by it. Even if prosperity comes to him, he has no desire for it).

—Samarth Ramdas

From now on, *Taai* would perhaps, not contest any elections! But then, it is just an interval. Her second innings has just begun! She has set an example on how to be an ideal politician although that was not her fundamental nature! Her basic nature is that of a *pravachankar*, teacher, scholar, preacher and thinker.

When *Taai* was awarded the Padma Bhushan, it was indeed a deserving honour, a great moment of joy and also increased many expectations from her.

The award was conferred on her by President Ram Nath Kovind at Rashtrapati Bhawan on November 9, 2021.

After receiving the Award, *Taai* said, "I am grateful to everyone for this honour. It feels like I have received recognition for my work of so many years.

"I am happy; Indore has been recognised. The love and support I received from volunteers and people of Indore, ethical upbringing by my father and strong support of my in- laws, have contributed towards my progress. The BJP also gave me the opportunity to work in different capacities and bestowed the responsibility of Speaker on me. With the support of everybody, I could handle the responsibility well. I have been rewarded for authenticity in public life."

"What advice you will give to the new generation of politicians?" asked one of the journalists. Sumitrataai replied, "Nobody can give advice to others. People learn from what they see and observe. You can achieve what you are destined to receive! God always helps if you honestly do whatever work is given to you and have a positive mind. When my party gives me any responsibility I strive to carry out the responsibility honestly. I believe in not expecting anything from life; that is why I have received so much. I feel blessed, I feel satisfied, I am contented!"

Millions of *Taai's* fans, volunteers in social field and future politicians are looking up to her with anticipation – they hope that she would offer suitable guidance in future. She will take ahead the ideological tradition of Chanakya, Samarth Ramdas, Pandit Deendayal Upadhyay and Shri Dattopant Thengdi. The serene, gentle and competent beacon of light would certainly guide the future generations on their journey towards clean politics.

□□□

Padma Bhushan Award Function	
https://economictimes.indiatimes.com/news/india/sumitra-mahajan-former-ls-speaker-awarded-padma-bhushan-says-her-work-has-been-recognised/videoshow/87605722.cms	